STRESS AND HOW TO MANAGE IT

TRANSFORMING TECHNIQUES TO PREVENT AND REDUCE EVERYDAY STRESS IN YOUR LIFE

LORI MAXWELL

CONTENTS

Introduction	ix
1. YOUR STRESSED-OUT BRAIN & BODY	1
Our Prehistoric Brains	3
What Is the Answer?	4
2. THE UP AND DOWNSIDES OF STRESS	13
Thoughts and Feelings	14
Eustress vs. Distress	17
Transforming Distress Into Eustress	19
3. OVERWHELMED!	25
Choose Simplicity	27
Choices	32
Focus	35
Distractions	38
Get Clear on What's Important	39
Create Boundaries and Maintain Them	41
4. RELEASING STRESS	45
Journaling	46
Music Therapy	47
Aromatherapy	50
Cryotherapy	52
Nature Baths	53
Movement	54
Affirmations & Visualizations	55
Meditation	57
Play and Laughter	59
Connection	59
5. HAVING A STRESSLESS LIFE	61
Frustration	62
Emotional Attachment Theory	64
The Power of Words and Stories	66

Watch Out for Thought Traps	69
Minding Your Habits	71

6. DEALING WITH STRESS AT WORK — 77
Finding Meaning — 78
Self-Management and Motivation — 80
Dealing With Conflict and Difficult People — 82

7. STRESS AT HOME — 85
Two Ears One Mouth — 86
Positive Parenting — 89
Top Conflicts — 92

8. DEALING WITH CHANGE — 95
Comfort Zones — 96
Building Resilience in a Changing Environment — 99

Conclusion — 101
References — 107
About the Author — 111

© Copyright 2022 - All rights reserved.

The content contained within this book may not be reproduced, duplicated or transmitted without direct written permission from the author or the publisher.

Under no circumstances will any blame or legal responsibility be held against the publisher, or author, for any damages, reparation, or monetary loss due to the information contained within this book, either directly or indirectly.

Legal Notice:

This book is copyright protected. It is only for personal use. You cannot amend, distribute, sell, use, quote or paraphrase any part, or the content within this book, without the consent of the author or publisher.

Disclaimer Notice:

Please note the information contained within this document is for educational and entertainment purposes only. All effort has been executed to present accurate, up to date, reliable, complete information. No warranties of any kind are declared or implied. Readers acknowledge that the author is not engaged in the rendering of legal, financial, medical or professional advice. The content within this book has been derived from various sources. Please consult a licensed professional before attempting any techniques outlined in this book.

By reading this document, the reader agrees that under no circumstances is the author responsible for any losses, direct or indirect, that are incurred as a result of the use of the information contained within this document, including, but not limited to, errors, omissions, or inaccuracies.

"Everyone has the ability to increase resilience to stress. It requires hard work and dedication, but over time, you can equip yourself to handle whatever life throws your way without adverse effects to your health. Training your brain to manage stress will not just affect the quality of your life, but perhaps even the length of it." ~ Amy Morin

INTRODUCTION

"When I hear somebody sigh, 'Life is hard,' I am always tempted to ask, 'Compared to what?'" - Sydney Harris.

It kinda creeps up on you! One minute you're young, and life is full of hope and excitement, and then next, you look around and the hall table is piled with unpaid bills; there are children in your house wanting all the things. Little Jimmy needs a new retainer, Jenny is going through her terrible threes and refuses to eat anything green, yellow, brown, or white; and the cat has just destroyed your new leather couch. That would all be fine, except your partner is late from work, nobody has started dinner, you are so tired you could creep under the bills and take a very long nap. Your boss just messaged to remind you about that last-minute report he gave you at 5 p.m. that he needs for an urgent presentation for the board first thing tomorrow. Not to mention, you are still upset over that snarky email that Roger in accounting sent you about your budget estimates. He even used capitals and copied your whole team. Just thinking about it again, you are steaming like a kettle.

INTRODUCTION

Great!

You know you signed up for the studies, career, work hours, partner, kids, house, and all that goes with it. Still, right now, you are wondering about the real meaning of life, where your head was at when you made all these decisions, and whether you should downsize and become an aromatherapy massage therapist. Except for Janet from the gym, she is a massage therapist and feels pretty stressed.

Let's face it; the reality is you can't have a meaningful life without a bit of struggle. Some downs are needed, so you know you when you experience ups. Everything (read absolutely everything) comes with both a good and bad side to it. That super-calm guru meditating on the mountain just had some ants bite his bottom, and that busy COO of a multinational just spent three months in the Azores on his yacht with only his dog for company and loads of champagne.

The thing is, there is no instruction manual given to us when we start out in life. Most of us find ourselves somehow getting through each day, and each day comes with new challenges, frustrations, and all kinds of stress. Like the frog in hot water, without us realizing it, our lives can heat up slowly, and we don't notice the temperature has reached boiling until at some point we crack, burn out, or end up having some kind of breakdown.

Many of us put our bodies and minds through a special kind of hell on a daily basis. We lead our bodies on a merry dance with overthinking, overcommitting, worrying, and getting frustrated. Racing heart rates, sweating and shaking, clenched jaws, hands, and aching muscles; upset stomachs and irritable bowels; nausea, and more, all follow the almost continual flood of stress chemicals through our systems. Every little (and big) thing starts to trigger us and releases more of these chemicals, which hang around in our bodies unprocessed more often than not. While our systems are programmed to fight off danger or run away from it, modern

INTRODUCTION

lifestyles and problems generally don't require us to do either of these things. And so, unwittingly, we pile up the stress in every cell and hardwire ourselves to become more reactive and vulnerable over time.

Ongoing, unmanaged stress is one of the leading causes of heart disease, diabetes, depression, anxiety, and a number of other unpleasant problems. And yet we can't avoid the things that often cause stress. They are going to happen, one way or another.

Before you book yourselves into the asylum or reserve a hospital bed, you need to know it does not need to be this way. You don't need to feel this bad all the time. And you certainly don't need to suffer from any of those nasty ailments we just mentioned. Even if you have been super stressed for quite some time, a new approach that brings some healing is possible.

You can't take all the challenges out of life, nor should you want to. Experiencing these challenges is how you learn, grow, and find stuff to pit yourself against. The satisfaction and reward of overcoming a hard time, and reaching a difficult goal, is a marvelous thing.

But there is a way of taking the sting out of all the stress. There is a way to reframe and redirect this stress energy into positive, constructive actions. And, more importantly, there is a way to achieve a (mostly) fabulous inner peace regardless of whatever life flings at you, no matter where you are or what is going on around you.

That sounds good, right? So, I thought I'd write you the instruction manual you should have had from the start. I'm keeping it simple. This book is your go-to for when you lose track. The tools and ideas will change how you look at yourself, others, and life in general.

The exercises can be done whenever you need to revisit a concept or repurpose yourself if you forget any of the great advice I'm about to give you. Before you know it, people will be asking

INTRODUCTION

you for your advice because you so clearly have it all together. Parenting, work, relationships, and running your household will settle into a smoother, more controllable rhythm. What I'm recommending is not some hard-sell, over-the-top promise. This stuff is really not hard. Some of it you probably already know. I'm just pulling it all together for you in a sensible way because that's what I like to do.

With a little bit of work now and then, you can have a completely different, more peaceful way of life.

So, let's begin.

1

YOUR STRESSED-OUT BRAIN & BODY

"Stressed is just desserts spelled backwards" - Loretta LaRoche.

As amusing as that may be, stress and dessert do have a bit to do with each other. Who does not find some level of comfort in food? We often associate it with love and happiness. And the irony is that those delicious, sweet desserts can actually raise stress levels in the end.

So many people look for answers to ill health, anxiety, and mood disorders, by going straight to the doctor and spending a lot of money on a bunch of supplements and medications. What they fail to realize is that unless your basic building blocks for health are in place, things like good sleep, a healthy diet, hydration, and sufficient exercise, the system can't work at its best.

All the studies point to the fact that excess sugars, fats, and chemical additives, as well as things like alcohol, are all pretty bad for us. Not just in the obvious ways, but in that these all lead to increased inflammation in the body and brain. This inflammation means our brains don't function as well as they could, directly affecting our mood. Anything that lowers the flow of oxygen to the brain, like high cholesterol, or smoking, also impacts brain function. Add to this poor nutrition in general, and our poor brains are even more challenged to keep things running as they have less of the things they need and more that needs doing with them. Neurogenesis (the creation of new brain cells) and the number of neurotransmitters needed for effective brain function suffers as a result. And again, our mood is impacted.

Why?

Well, let's look at this very simply. Our brains are weird sacs of fat, liquids, chemicals, salts, and although this sounds pretty straightforward, all of these elements need to operate in complex ways in order to produce our thoughts and drive our entire systems, keeping us alive. In there we find a range of chemicals that drive mood, like serotonin (regulates mood), oxytocin (the love hormone, warm, nurturing, connected, trusting), dopamine (creates pleasurable feelings that help with motivation and learning), and endorphins (brief euphoria, pain-killing). Our brain also triggers the release of stress chemicals, mainly from our adrenal glands, like adrenaline and cortisol. These hormones constrict blood vessels, send blood pumping madly around your body, release extra sugars, shut down digestion and non-essential functions, and generally prepare you to fight or run away in the face of danger. Our biology is what creates our emotions, whether they are good or bad.

Of course, our thoughts can also influence our biology, which then creates an emotion too. But we will deal with that later.

What you need to know for now is that any imbalance in these various vital chemicals and neurotransmitters in our system and brains can throw the whole thing out of whack. And a full range of poor lifestyle choices certainly can do this.

Anything that negatively affects, inflames, and dysregulates our bodies will affect our brains, and thus our mood. It confuses and creates chaos in a complex system. And this can become serious (read chronic) when it is an ongoing thing. That is one of the ways we end up with a variety of cognitive problems because we have been putting garbage into our supercomputers and then getting garbage out.

You need to get really clear on that if you genuinely want to start making a difference to your quality of life and inner calm.

OUR PREHISTORIC BRAINS

For some reason, our brains haven't changed an awful lot since the days we were happily frolicking around the plains, living in caves, and making Flintstone's impressions. In those crazy days, we had fairly simple, straightforward lives. We had to hunt, gather, stay warm, and stay alive. I'm sure that prehistoric people had their own varieties of stress when the seasons were hard, and food wasn't plentiful, for example. Mainly what they needed to survive was to either fight (hunt, fight off a grizzly bear, or whatever) or run away really fast. They also needed to be able to freeze in the shadows so that danger couldn't see them too easily. Added to that, the guy who spent his time looking at rainbows and pretty flowers generally got eaten or fell down a hole, and the ones who paid attention to that shaking in the bush, which could be a ravenous beast or that feeling of danger in the dark, tended to survive.

So our brains and bodies are still operating in those settings.

Now let's fast-forward to modern times. There are a lot of potential stressors to be found in most people's daily lives. Very few of these will actually kill us, but our brains (on a functional level) don't know this, even if we logically do. Each time a horn hoots, a siren wails, the traffic gets crazy, your boss acts up, or your toddler has a meltdown, you go on high alert mentally, which triggers your body to set the whole fight-freeze-flight process in motion. Our bodies flood with stress chemicals, and because we don't actually have to fight or run away, they just hang around in our systems, clogging up the works. Add to that how we are programmed to watch for danger (that results in a negative bias to our powers of observation and thoughts), and the sheer number of things that can trigger us in a day, we end up with a body that is almost always on high alert. Do this for long enough, and our systems get pretty fatigued. Our adrenal glands burn out due to overwork, our sugar levels are all over the place, our digestion suffers, our weight fluctuates, and those stress chemicals build up and don't leave for long. Our bodies adapt as much as they can, but this means that we eventually become hardwired for stress, reactive, jumpy, tired, and so on.

Our bodies are set up to process a wide variety of foods, mainly nuts, seeds, grains, legumes, fruits, and vegetables, plus whatever protein in the form of eggs, insects, and small mammals that could be found day-to-day. Larger quantities of meat happened after a successful hunt, which certainly wasn't an everyday thing. Dairy only came later, when humankind settled and started farming, which may be why many of us don't handle it so well. This is also why we have problems when we flood our bodies with extra sugars and other manufactured chemicals that our bodies don't recognize and don't know what to do with.

No wonder modern lifestyles and stress are one of the leading health disasters of our modern age.

The added stress of the Covid pandemic years (plus widespread changes to earning and income, lifestyle, and personal freedom) has led to a massive upsurge in people suffering from sleeplessness, anxiety, depression, and other chronic mood disorders.

WHAT IS THE ANSWER?

Taking into account everything we just discovered, managing our stress levels starts with checking our basics. Are we putting the right kind of fuel into our vehicles, and is it perhaps not time for a tune-up?

Yes, I get it. The healthy living crowd has been going on about this stuff for decades, and the thought of high-fiber, tasteless cereals, boring salads, health shakes, and leg warmers puts many of us to sleep.

It is not about that, though. You can be pretty healthy in your own way, eating the foods you love, and still nail it. I find a mindful approach to life helps. Each bite or sip I take first gets a conscious decision. Am I prepared to do this to my body? Is there a better choice I could make right now? Am I treating myself to this thing within reason? These are all good questions to keep in your mind so that you start making better choices on average.

It also helps to be mindful of the other stuff. When your mood is low or anxious, check-in with yourself. Have I been sleeping well? Have I been outdoors and felt some sun on my face and the wind in my hair lately? Have I moved from my office chair much today? These are also part of the vital building blocks that contribute to a healthy body, brain, and good mood.

It is funny that we do this automatically for little kids. When a small child is crying or acting up, we check that they aren't tired, hungry, ill, in pain, too hot or cold, thirsty, and so on. And yet we don't extend the same thinking to ourselves? And we really need to. When our mood is off, that should be the first thing we do before we start looking for someone, or some situation, to blame for our emotions.

So let's see what a check-up and tune-up involves.

Practical Exercise: Check-in and Tune-Up

1. How are you sleeping? Take a moment to rate yourself on the following areas:
2. Have you done any activity, enough to feel physically tired, today? If you are sitting at a desk 24/7, your body isn't using up excess energy, and you may struggle to sleep.
3. Is your bedroom quiet and undisturbed? Is there any light, or noise, at night? Can you put up blackout curtains, use white noise, or put simple soundproofing (like thicker curtains, wall hangings, carpets, or even a double-layer door) in place? Noise and light can wake the soundest sleeper.
4. Is your bed comfortable? Is it warm enough, clean, and soft? Does it smell nice? Does your mattress support your body and back adequately, and stop any bed partners movements from disturbing you?
5. Is your sleepwear comfortable and loose?
6. Did you eat any large meals right before bed? If so, that can interfere with restful sleep as your body tries to digest it. Instead, stick to smaller snacks in the last few hours before bed.
7. Were you watching TV on your computer or cellphone in the last hour before bed? That is a recipe for disaster. The light emitted from most screens fools our bodies into producing less melatonin (sleep hormone), and also, the activity wakes up our brains, so we take longer to fall asleep. Try stopping at least an hour before you plan to sleep and use blue-light filters on your screens at night.
8. Do you have a wind-down routine? Any combination of warm drinks, showering or bathing, stretches, journaling, reading, meditation or prayer, or whatever quiet activity you like, done in a familiar pattern every night primes your brain and body for a good night's rest.

After a hot bath or shower, your body goes into a cool-down, which can be very relaxing. As can, some light yoga stretches or just lying with your legs up against a wall.

1. What temperature is your bedroom? Experts advise around 18 to 19 degrees celsius is best for sleep for adults. Small babies need it a bit warmer. If you are in a hot climate, you may need a ceiling fan or air conditioner, and cold climates may need warm, goose-down duvets or even inside heating to achieve this.
2. Did you get enough sleep? Sleep can vary quite widely from person to person, but a good indication is that you wake up feeling refreshed and not still tired. Try a simple sleep reset if you often wake in the night and battle to fall asleep again. Get out of bed, sit quietly somewhere with dim light, and either read, journal, or do something fairly calm. Then when you feel drowsy again, go back to bed. Whatever you do, do not reach for your mobile phone and start scrolling.

How did you answer these sleep checks? What could you improve today in your sleep space, and what do you need to plan and save to do? Make a list.

1. What did you eat and drink today? Making healthier choices is not rocket science. You can slowly replace any unhealthy choices with better ones. Don't rush it too much, or you may toss the whole idea.
2. Did you drink a lot of sugary sodas and coffees, or did you choose water, herbal teas, and fruit or vegetable smoothies and soups?
3. Did you go for a wide variety of foods and food colors? Have you included something from all the food groups in

your day? Go for nuts, seeds, whole grains, fatty fish, lean meats, fruits, vegetables, and legumes. Steer away from hydrogenated oils (like reused cooking oils used to deep fry, for example), and include healthy seed oils instead.

4. Did you eat a lot of sugary treats? You can cut back slowly on added sugars or replace them with a natural sweetener like xylitol and you might find that your taste buds start revolting at overly sweet stuff eventually. The flavors of food in its natural state become more delicious too. This does not mean you can't ever have cookies, sweets, and desserts, just that you have these in moderation and in a much smaller amount as compared to the other healthier stuff. Many berries, fruits, or even dark chocolate can provide a sweet treat and be more nutritious than processed sweets. In most supermarkets, you will find sweet alternatives in the diabetic/health aisles.

5. Did you eat a lot of processed stuff full of refined flours and chemical additives? Try to include food in its raw or unprocessed state more often, except for meats, of course. Read food labels, buy from health-conscious suppliers, and beware that "healthy" on a label can still be unhealthy. Many "healthy" drinks and things like sports drinks, energy bars, and so on are actually full of some pretty unhealthy stuff.

6. Did you think about your poor, overworked gut? All the studies are in and support the fact that an inflamed, unhealthy gut has a direct impact on mood. Cutting out sugars and additives and adding probiotics in supplement or food form can go a long way to helping lift your moods long term.

7. Did you include any good-mood foods in your day?

Bananas, berries, nuts and seeds, fatty fish high in omega 3s, oats, and even coffee (easy on the sugar) can help lift a struggling mood. Probiotic food like yogurt, kefir, kimchi, sauerkraut, and food high in B vitamins, like poultry, eggs, and leafy greens, are also great for this. These foods help your body and brain produce more of the feel-good chemicals and neurotransmitters needed.

Getting your diet right can take time and patience. Slowly find healthier choices that you can enjoy, and replace old food habits one at a time. Make each bite a conscious choice. Be aware of what you are eating and track it on a food tracking app if need be. A little advance planning, keeping easy-to-prepare snacks and light meals in the kitchen, and packing snacks for the road, can also help you avoid those binge moments when you make all the wrong choices because your hunger has spiraled out of control.

1. Did you move at all today? Not all of us dig exercise, but moving your body around does not need to mean spending hours at the gym in embarrassing workout clothes. What kind of movement repels you the least? Some people like walks or hikes in nature, which serves as a double mood booster as nature is also a great way to lift your spirits. Other people like dancing or more strenuous stuff. It does not matter what you choose, just don't sit around all day long. Even if you are working at a screen, get up every half hour, take a walk, or do some stretches or a few pushups, pullups or any form of physical activity.

Movement serves a dual purpose. It lifts your mood as effectively as many medications in the longer term, with fewer side effects. Around 20 - 30 minutes of brisk physical activity about three times a week is enough to maintain this. It is the number one way to work stress chemicals out of your system faster in the short term. So the next time you get upset, worried, or reactive, take a walk or do some star jumps or whatever it takes. Do it as soon as possible after you notice the signs that you are feeling out of sorts. The sooner you clear your body of unnecessary stress chemicals, the better. This approach also helps with longer-term body and brain healing and helps reverse that stress hardwiring we spoke about before.

1. Try to cut out or down on the obvious no-nos. A little red wine is good for you, but too much alcohol contains a lot of sugar and other stuff that inflames our systems. Smoking reduces oxygen to the brain. These are no-brainers, in that no, your brain does not do as well with them around.
2. Lastly, are you feeling a bit allergic? Allergy sufferers have an increase in cytokines in the system that inflames soft tissue and, you guessed it, the brain. To help relieve bad moods, keeping your allergies in check by reducing sugar, working on gut health, and taking anti-inflammatory supplements are all good ideas.

After running through this list, what can you start doing more of, and less of, right now? Add it to your health plan. If you are unsure, keep a record of it all for about a week to get a clear idea of what's going on internally. We are often so unconscious about this stuff that we only realize how much we have let things slip if we physically track it in real-time. Keep a notebook on you and note: the date, what you ate, drank, or supplemented, any medications you take, activity levels, and your mood that day. After you have enough data, analyze it critically to get an accurate idea of what is going on.

If you suspect that you have been struggling with stress over an extended period of time, then the odds are your adrenal glands may be a bit overworked. If you are tired all the time, dehydrated, have foggy thinking, weight loss, weakness, dizziness, low blood pressure, diarrhea, and vomiting, these may all be linked to adrenal fatigue. It is best to get this properly diagnosed by your general practitioner (GP).

Chronic stress may also present as unexplained aches and pains, sleeplessness, frequent infections and illnesses, irritability, randomly fluctuating moods, and disorganized thinking.

All the things mentioned in this section will contribute towards chronic stress and adrenal healing, and there are also a few supplements you could consider.

- Pro- and prebiotics for gut health.
- Calcium.
- Magnesium.
- Essential fatty acids, specifically Omega 3s. Look for the EPA rating on the side of the bottle, because around 1000 EPA is a good daily goal for mood elevation.
- Valerian is a herbal calmative that you can use in milder doses in the day, and higher doses for sleeping.
- L-theanine.
- Chamomile tea is also great for general calm.
- B vitamins.
- Vitamin D and C.
- 5-HTP which is a precursor, or building block, for serotonin. (Nazario, 2021)

There are many other supplements, as well as over-the-counter, and prescribed medications that are available. Always consult your GP and discuss a holistic treatment plan. Make sure they know about all the other supplements you currently take or have tried.

By putting some effort into your basics and staying mindful of how you maintain this, you make it so much more likely that a good mood will follow. Of course, there is more than that to this issue, but that is definitely one of the key factors. Ignore it at your peril.

2

THE UP AND DOWNSIDES OF STRESS

"Stress acts as an accelerator: it will push you either forward or backward, but you choose which direction." —Chelsea Erieau.

Many people live day to day with a relatively consistent level of stress about what each day contains. Stress such as bills, the kids acting up, your partner being demanding or moody, and the costly appliances keep breaking. Then you have work where your colleagues are playing at some hidden agenda, the economy is shaky, the company is faced with potential ruin, and the daily commute is simply mind-numbingly awful.

This scenario is not unique. Most of us face a large variety of challenges all the time. And those things are likely to continue throughout our lives in one form or another. So why does one person breeze through life, and the next fold under the pressure? If you were to compare them, you might say, "Oh, but she has it so easy, and he had a much harder run." But how do we know that for sure? Appearances are deceptive. Everyone's experience of the world is so different. Everyone's resilience and strength are on a different level.

The real reason why some people do better, mentally and emotionally, is because they have learned some basic coping skills. They have built up resilience and fortitude that helps them when life gets tough.

Sadly, these coping skills are mostly learned in a hit-and-miss manner. Most schooling systems, and many families, do not teach what is needed to learn how to process and manage thoughts and feelings in order to be more resilient. So we tend to learn through the school of hard knocks, mostly. There is no cohesive understanding of how to get there otherwise.

I once heard a great explanation of this problem. Our minds are like sharp knives. We are handed one at birth, but nobody shows us how to use this tool. So we hold it by the wrong end and end up cutting ourselves with it.

So let's cover the basic understanding that we should have already been given. In learning how to use our minds safely, we can change the plot and give it a better ending.

THOUGHTS AND FEELINGS

At the outset, all we know is that we feel bad. We are overwhelmed, anxious, can't stop worrying, hyperalert, and feel like we are constantly under some form of attack. How do we start unraveling this knotty situation?

It helps to know how we got there.

Before we begin to feel something, our bodies have to release certain chemicals into our systems. We covered that in the last chapter. We first need to think about a series of thoughts to release those chemicals. To think those thoughts, we need to first be in a specific context, such as the stressful situation, and also pick what thoughts we will think; this is where we can make a real difference to how we feel, at the level of that decision.

Most of us decide automatically. We each have a relatively

unique set of ideas around what the world consists of and what it's all about. Sure there will at times be a common, shared way of thinking, but once you realize that each person has a necessity of different genes, a different experience of the world from the moment of conception, and then will formulate their own thoughts based on that, you will understand that while we may be the same in many ways, we are also very different.

Added to our biology are what sort of family group and culture we adapt to; what our parents teach us, caregivers, family, teachers, and friends; and how we interpret and respond to each experience. This builds up into a worldview that we quite often unconsciously hold. This worldview helps us make decisions about each new experience, decides our quality of thoughts, and determines what we feel next.

This is why when the exact same thing happens to two different people; we will get two different reactions and interpretations. One may get stressed, and another might laugh it off.

The problem is, we don't stop and look into the nature of these thoughts when we start feeling bad. Instead of understanding that a feeling is a messenger indicating something is either not working in our thoughts or our environment or both, we think our feelings are an end result. We believe our feelings are who we are, our identity, or that they are inevitable. We also tend to think that our feelings are true, when in fact, if our thoughts are misled or misguided in various ways, then it stands to reason that our feelings will also be flawed and misleading. This is why making big life decisions based on our feelings alone is often not such a great idea. We first need to step back and get a bird's eye view of all the facts, our reactions, thoughts, and the resulting feelings to understand what really might be going on and what the next best step may be.

The best way to do so is:

- Delay a decision or action/reaction until you are ready.

This can involve asking for more time, walking away temporarily, or just learning to count to 10 and take some time. It may feel uncomfortable at first, especially if you are a person who gets things done fast, but over time you will feel at ease with this approach and see the benefits.

- Identify what you are feeling. Put a name to it. If you are not used to this, a great way to define feelings is using the emoji range or a one-pager feelings chart (there are lots online) with emoji faces linked to feeling labels. We often use these to teach small children about their feelings, but so many of us have grown up disconnected from our feelings that it can help us immensely at any age to learn this skill.
- Identify your thoughts about the situation right before your feelings kick in. Write them down if you need to.
- Now step back mentally, and question each of these thoughts. How do you know this to be true? Are there more facts you can find? Who can you ask? Where can you look? Is there another way to think about this? Is there a more helpful or constructive way to think about this thing?
- Only at this stage are you perhaps ready to decide your next steps.

Over time you may realize that some of your thoughts are particularly negative or unhelpful. This realization then opens up the way to shifting these thought patterns. But first, you need to become aware of both your feelings and the thoughts behind them. An excellent way to track this is to carry a small notebook and pencil or use your mobile phone to record your feelings, underlying thoughts, and the preceding events each time something goes wrong in your life. Do this for at least a week to better picture what is happening in your head. At times like these, we will see a lot of automatic, reactive thinking come up, and it is easier to pick up unhelpful thought patterns that may be contributing to your stress levels.

The main learning you need to get from this is that what happens in our world is not responsible for how we feel. What we choose to think about it is at the root of the resulting emotion. Our emotions can add up into a stressed state and then decide the choices and actions we take.

We can take the same life and events and tweak our thoughts sufficiently so that we have a whole different and better experience regardless of what is happening in our outer world. Becoming the observer and detective of our thoughts is key to managing our emotions.

EUSTRESS VS. DISTRESS

As with most things in life, stress operates on a spectrum. At one end, we have people who use the energy of challenges to help motivate and drive useful actions. At the other end of the spectrum are those who cannot process or cope and end up with severe anxiety, panic attacks, etc.

Distress is stress that negatively affects you, and eustress has a more positive, motivating effect. When several potentially stressful things happen simultaneously, eustress can also transform into distress.

Of course, certain situations are potentially more negatively stressful than others. There are several stress scales that help us quantify this. The Rahe scale gives stress points to certain major life events.

1. Death of spouse = 100
2. Divorce = 73

3. Marital separation = 65
4. Jail term = 63
5. Death of close family member = 63
6. Personal injury or illness = 53
7. Marriage = 50
8. Fired at work = 47
9. Marital reconciliation = 45
10. Retirement = 45
11. Change in health of family member = 44
12. Pregnancy = 40
13. Sex difficulties = 39
14. Gain of new family member = 39
15. Business readjustment = 39
16. Change in financial state = 38
17. Death of close friend = 37
18. Change to a different line of work = 36
19. Change in number of arguments with spouse = 35
20. A large mortgage or loan = 31
21. Foreclosure of mortgage or loan = 30
22. Change in responsibilities at work = 29
23. Son or daughter leaving home = 29
24. Trouble with in-laws = 29
25. Outstanding personal achievement =28
26. Spouse begins or stops work = 26
27. Begin or end school/college = 26
28. Change in living conditions = 25
29. Revision of personal habits = 24
30. Trouble with boss = 23
31. Change in work hours or conditions = 20
32. Change in residence = 20
33. Change in school/college = 20
34. Change in recreation = 19
35. Change in church activities = 19

36. Change in social activities = 18
37. A moderate loan or mortgage = 17
38. Change in sleeping habits = 16
39. Change in number of family get-togethers = 15
40. Change in eating habits = 15
41. Vacations = 13
42. Christmas = 12
43. Minor violations of the law = 11 (Rahe, 1967).

If you score yourself against these factors, and if your combined (added up) score is between 11 and 150, you have a low to moderate chance of experiencing health-related stress symptoms. From 150 to 299, you have a moderate to high risk, and 300 to 600 is the danger zone where they predict you will need more immediate assistance with the problem.

This is all very well, but as we already know, we each respond differently to specific stressors. It is very much to do with your state of mind and quality of your thoughts around each event, your existing coping skills, plus how much you are dealing with at one go (complexity), and your physical health (tolerance levels), that altogether decides how much distress or eustress (positive stress) you may feel.

TRANSFORMING DISTRESS INTO EUSTRESS

When life presents a challenge, we can be excited, motivated, and energized to meet the challenge, solve the problem, and keep going. Alternatively, we can allow ourselves to get lost in fears and frustration and allow stress to master us. Naturally, not every challenge is going to be exciting. They can also be sad, boring, repetitive, or traumatic because some stuff is like that. You are not going to feel great when a loved one dies, or you are involved in a car accident, for example. There are different coping methods to use for this big stuff that I will share later.

But the small and medium-sized stressors, like a difficult coworker or boss, a kid acting out, or the monthly bills, can definitely be managed differently. If we can get into the habit of reframing this stuff and learning to manage our responses and choices better, over time, we will find ourselves in generally a stronger, better, less distressed frame of mind.

It is not what we feel but how we decide to proceed that will make the difference here. Like many difficult feelings, the sensation of stress can be flipped and used as powerful energy rather than a destructive force.

First, we need to recognize that we are stressed. What are the immediate signs to notice this straight away?

- Elevated heart rate. A feeling that your heart is pounding or racing.
- Elevated rate of breathing.
- Clenched jaw, hands, or other muscles.
- Aching jaw or muscles.
- Abdominal discomfort, diarrhea, or nausea.
- Sweating.
- Flushed skin or face.
- Shaking.
- Headache or dizziness.
- Racing thoughts.
- Irritability.
- Problems concentrating.
- A sudden need to enact certain behaviors to self-soothe. Any compulsive behavior.

These are not the long-term effects, but some of the immediate, main signals that signify that you may be in a stressed state right now. We don't need to experience all of them; even one indicator is enough to show we are possibly stressing. These reactions mean something has happened, and you have already decided on some level that there is a threat. You can't go back in time and change those initial thoughts right now, but you can take better control from here.

You first need to acknowledge that you are indeed stressed, and then your new awareness will allow you to do something a little different.

- Remind yourself that your body is simply showing it is ready for action. It is flooded with chemicals that prime it (and you) to do something right now.
- Drop the negative interpretation of this physical state. This is you having a natural biological response. See this as pure energy that will help you if you use it right.
- Ask yourself what activity will be helpful at this moment. It does not need to be directly related to the source of the stress reaction. For example:
- Get going on something you have been putting off.
- Complete a project or chore.
- Use the energy to power your exercise.
- Once you have determined a helpful activity, go ahead and get started on it. Mindfully pour all that excess energy into the task you have chosen. If your mind wants to wander off into the past or future, gently but firmly bring it back to what is presently at hand.
- When you are back in control of your mind and body, if you feel able, you can examine your root thoughts and the situation that led you to feel stressed to see what else or what you could do differently. Separating the source of your stress from the actual stress you feel helps immensely with processing and reducing your

overall stress levels. You may not be able to do much about the stress source right now, but you have the power to do a lot about your current state of being.

In order to transform distress into eustress at the root before you even hit the full fight-or-flight situation, a better long-term approach would require that you:

- Ensure your self-care regime is on track as much as possible. This includes all the things mentioned in the previous chapter. If you are not physically strong enough, everything will feel much harder to accomplish, so this is your first step.
- Engage with your feelings and thoughts. Observe them and analyze them. Use your feelings as messengers and not facts in and of themselves. See where unhelpful thoughts can be rephrased or reframed towards a more constructive, helpful outlook.
- In the moment of stress, redefine your view of stress itself. See the signs of stress as an indication that your body is full of energy right now, and channel that energy into a useful action rather than letting yourself sit, stew, and overthink yourself into a stress coma.

Not everything can be transformed on the spot. There will be times when bad things happen, and it simply is what it is. But you will learn to judge these more accurately as time goes by. If you are in the habit of monitoring your thoughts and channeling stress energy for all the little things, when bigger things occur, you will find this habit supports you through those too.

Practical Exercise: A Stress Self-Analysis

Let's take a quick snapshot of where you are at stress-wise right now.

- Look back at the immediate signs of stress. How often in a day do you feel any of these things?
- Would you say you are more reactive (acting on impulse, without much thought first) or responsive (taking time to consider an action carefully)?
- How often in a day do you feel?
- Frustrated.
- Overwhelmed.
- Worried.
- Anxious.
- Panicked.
- Fearful.
- Angry.
- Pressurized.
- Confused.
- Guilty or ashamed.
- Disconnected or numb.

If your answer to any of these questions is yes, and often, then your stress levels are likely quite high. In this case, it is imperative that you destress fast. Use any of the physical fixes in the last chapter, and start acting on the path to a more peaceful life with the exercises in this book. I hope you aren't skipping any.

3

OVERWHELMED!

"And every day, the world will drag you by the hand, yelling, "This is important! And this is important! And this is important! You need to worry about this! And this! And this!" And each day, it is up to you to yank your hand back, put it on your heart and say, "No. This is what's important." —
Iain Thomas

Imagine yourself as a balloon. Every puff of air added to you is some extra to-do, responsibility, worry, or other complexity of life. The more air inserted, the bigger you expand, internal pressure builds up, and the more the outer barrier stretches. If too much air is added, at some point, the balloon will tear and rupture at its own unique weak spot and pop.

Just like these over-inflated balloons, our lives will rupture wherever we are weakest. The rupture may result in depression, alcohol abuse, illness, substance abuse, panic attacks, or any form of physical, emotional, or mental breakdown and disorder imaginable. It all depends on where we are most fragile. But no matter the end result, the root cause is all that climbing pressure that bursts our balloons.

Think about how our lives and lifestyles have changed in the last century alone. While humankind has always had many things to worry about, these days, our modern world has new elements that make life even more complex than usual.

We are dealing with:

- A time of rapid development and change. If you are standing still, it is said, then you are actually going in reverse compared to everyone else.
- Everything is faster—transport, technology, work and income-production, banking, communication, and more.
- We are all connected to various devices that keep us switched on at all times. Even in the middle of the night when we should be sleeping, many of us are scrolling through reams of information on our mobile devices, placed next to our beds.
- We are constantly overstimulated by data. Advertisements, ongoing worldwide news (that we often can do little about), insights, movies, series, games, clickbait, instant messages, social media platforms, and all other forms of online information and entertainment bombard us daily.
- In a consumer-driven economy, we are spammed and flooded with continual adverts, many of which use fear to sell things to us. Fear of looking bad, not knowing enough, failing, getting ill, losing money, being socially rejected, or losing status or other resources drives us to make purchases that generally don't do anything to alleviate that fear. They just keep ramping it up.

Just because we can physically do so much more in a day than we could 100 years ago does not mean that we should. Sure, our employers may push for that 150%, and as long as money is their highest value, employees will be squeezed for every drop of energy we have.

But not everyone operates this way, and more people are awakening to the fact that this always-on, on-the-go, hectic lifestyle is unwise psychologically, physically, and socially. There is a return to the need to slow down, simplify, and refocus on more lasting and meaningful values than speed and money.

It is time to stop trading our sanity and health for our to-do lists. Our brains simply cannot keep up with the demands we place on them.

Take, for example, a baby or small child. Most parents will know that when that child suddenly gets a fixed look and starts to cry, it is probably time for a nap. The child may have been having a great time up until that point, and there is no real reason for the breakdown, except that a lot has been happening, and they are simply overstimulated. It is time for the brain to take a break to process all the recent input, and this is best done while sleeping, or perhaps with a quiet time in the bath or cuddled with a parent in a calm, quiet spot.

But as adults, we schedule a bunch of things for ourselves. We seldom leave any downtime in our plans. Our days are jam-packed with activities and responsibilities, many cups of coffee, a lot of to-do lists, stacks of people to speak to or see, and so on. We don't stop to think that as fabulous as our brains are, they still need some quiet time to process all this input. If we don't give ourselves some simple calm in our days, we will certainly be headed for a meltdown. It may not be the tantrum a small child throws, but it will feel just as bad on the inside.

CHOOSE SIMPLICITY

When you feel like you are drowning and overwhelmed in stress, one of the first things to do to calm it all down is to simplify.

Taking a moment to declutter your life wherever possible will provide an instant feeling of relief and ease.

You may think that it is too difficult or that you have responsibilities you just can't drop. Perhaps you feel that no one will do as good a job as you? This is often the mindset of a perfectionist. Let me tell you, under that burning need to get everything right lurks a lot of fear. Sit with that for a bit, if this is you. If you can face and understand these fears, you will be able to let go of the inexorable need to do it all yourself. And, as a result, you wind yourself into an ever-tightening, suffocating web of to-dos.

It also helps to let go of what other people may or may not think to simplify life. For years I held myself to impossible deadlines, so I know what I'm talking about. The hilarious (not-so hilarious) thing about this time of my life was that, more often than not, I was the one to set the deadlines. Then I would stress when I couldn't meet them. It probably didn't even feature as a blip on the radar for other people. What I eventually learned was that at any time, if I was feeling under the hammer, I could reorganize, reschedule, and take a breather. Nobody actually minded except me.

When and if you have kids, this always-on mentality worsens. You get into a rhythm of perpetually doing, like some sort of perpetual motion machine. At some point, you find that when you try to sit down, take five and relax, you somehow have lost the ability to do so. A five-minute bath is the most you can do. After a few minutes of watching a series or reading a book, you feel an irresistible urge to get up and do something. And believe me, it is pretty easy to find a hundred little chores to do if you are a family person.

Added to that is this weird work ethic that some of us have. It also has to do with constant motion. If you are staring off into space, thinking, that does not look like work from the outside. You are expected, by yourself or others, to be constantly doing something in order to be considered productive. This is honestly the biggest load of bovine excrement I have ever heard. It is easy to look busy but not be doing anything useful at all. But this approach is not that productive unless you work on an actual production line. And even then, a human being has to stop and rest occasionally.

A good rule of thumb is around 10 minutes off for every hour on whatever it is you are doing. For most adults, we can concentrate for around half an hour intently, or up to an hour less intently, before we need a break.

You need to cut yourself some slack!

There are some quick and easy ways to simplify your life fairly quickly. This can be an interim measure while you rest and recuperate or a longer-term way of life. My zen friends like to remind me often that we are human "beings," not human "doings". Even though I think I have slowed right down, apparently, I still look quite frenetic from time to time to the rest of the world.

Firstly, look at your current time commitments. What can be delayed or rescheduled? What can be delegated to someone else to do? What can you drop off the schedule altogether? What is the worst that can happen if you do any of these things?

Look, some stuff is both urgent and important, like going to your kids' school concert or getting that doctor's check-up because you have been having those palpitations again. This stuff needs to be kept in your diary if at all possible. But there are other things that appear urgent (often to others), like your Mom's tenth phone call today, but in reality, are not that important. This stuff can often be dropped altogether. Although you do need to stay in touch with your parents, it does not need to be every day unless there is an emergency. Creating healthy boundaries is a big part of teaching the world how much of your time you are willing to give them. Then there are the important things that aren't so urgent, like getting your annual dental check-up. This stuff can happen anytime you have a gap in your schedule. Don't put it off forever, as it is important to do, but you can defer it until later.

Create some breathing space for yourself. Get accustomed to asking for help. Get used to allowing others to do things for you, with you, and for themselves. For starters, allowing others to do things means you don't have to do them. This also lets other people feel good about themselves. They will feel seen and recognized. They will feel empowered and more confident. They will be happy because they can help you.

It does not matter that they will not do it the same way you would have. Suppose it is an ongoing and important task; you could delegate with a bit of guidance if needed. If it is not a make-or-break deal, and your partner is not wiping the counter, or bathing the dog, exactly the way you like it, that is something you could let go of. Truly. For those who battle with this, a good way to do it is simply not to play quality control. To hand over the task and at that moment mentally detach from it and put your focus on other important stuff instead. Strongly resist that urge to check, comment, or control what you have handed off to someone else. No matter how you feel about it, I promise your way isn't the only acceptable way.

Another stumbling block to simplifying our lives is pride. So many of us are reluctant, or too proud, to ask for assistance or to reschedule. But if you put yourself in the other person's shoes, you will realize that they don't feel negatively about you. If you have ever been allowed to help another person, doesn't that usually leave you feeling good about yourself? Just so! And as for rescheduling, I would far rather be given an accurate timeline for a project or event and be promptly communicated with if anything changes rather than be told at the last minute that it can't happen or see a colleague or friend collapse from the strain.

STRESS AND HOW TO MANAGE IT

Practical Exercise: Decluttering Your Life

Sit quietly with a pen and paper, and brainstorm all the things stressing you out right now. Now calmly consider what you can do about each one.

Can you drop, delegate, or defer it?

What is the worst thing that can happen? What might the repercussions be? Do these things matter at all? Will it matter in five days or five years? If these unfortunate consequences do happen, what can be done at that point?

Once you have made the decision, take action. Communicate with whoever you need to rearrange things. If they push back with unreasonable demands, simply ask them for their reasoning behind insisting on certain things or timelines. When faced with reason, calm, and logic, many people will back down if they can't provide a reasonable justification for their reaction. If you also explain how you are feeling and the effects of this stress on you, most people will be more than understanding. In the end, a simple, calm "no" is a lovely word to use, too.

You should be feeling a lot better already, having done all of this.

To level up the decluttering even further, take a look at your life holistically.

Are there any physical possessions you can get rid of, give away, or sell? If you haven't used a thing for over a year, do you need it cluttering up your space? This extends to visual clutter around your office or home, which can be very distracting to the eye and brain. Also, cluttered storage spaces, desktops, and directory trees on your computer system, and so on, can be slowly decluttered as you go. Put it into a plan, and cross off each item or step as you go. It does not all have to happen at once. Remember, we are trying to declutter and destress, not add to the burden. Are there any people in your life who are more of a drain than a delight? Can you not spend so much time around them or on them?

Are there any habits you have that serve no practical purpose but instead leave you feeling tired? Can you replace these with something more meaningful or useful?

Are there any unhelpful thoughts cluttering up your mind? Can you let go of those? Can you forgive, take the lesson, apologize, analyze, or take whatever action is needed so that you can put them in your permanent archives.

Once you have decluttered and simplified, resist the urge to fill up the spare time you have created for as long as possible. Leave that open, and use it to rest, recharge, or pursue something out of choice and not duty.

CHOICES

Part of life's complexity is that we are overwhelmed by choices these days. We have numerous decisions to make throughout the day, and after a while, we start feeling anxious, stressed, irritable, and even numb. This phenomenon has been diagnosed as an endemic lifestyle issue common to modern times. This is decision fatigue at a level our forefathers have not experienced.

A generation or two ago, life was a lot slower. Technology, population escalation, resource availability, and globalization have sped things up and widened our horizons in great but startling ways. We can go more places, do more things, and have a vast array of entertainment, products, and services to choose from as well. Now we know about what is happening all over the world, and it all has an impact on us; even knowledge of the stuff going on far away raises our overall stress levels. What happens in a country far from us could impact our local petrol and food prices, raise the cost of needed imports or reduce income from exports, and the cost of living is impacted. Not only that but we are deluged by advertising asking us to choose between a vast range for every item we use. We also need to make ordinary life choices such as What to study, where to study, who to spend time with, what to do for a living, and more. These choices are seldom once-off like in the past. Nowadays, it is accepted and expected that people will regularly change jobs, careers, skill sets, living locations, and even partners.

Having choices is great on many levels. It creates options, freedom, and healthy supplier competition too. But this also all adds up to many things we have to decide.

Our brains are not set up for so much choice. We can even track this on fMRI brain scans. Our frontal lobes are our decision-making centers, and we can see this section firing away and also growing fatigued over time. We can link our ability to make decisions and see how it deteriorates pretty quickly when we have to make a lot of them in one go. It does not seem to matter what size the decisions are so much as the number of them. Studies in court rulings show even judges making life-and-death decisions start out doing well, decline until around lunchtime, perk up slightly after the rest, but tend to make a lot less favorable decisions as the day proceeds (Clear, n.d).

A simple study by Professor Sheena Iyengar at Columbia University shows how this impacts on something as simple as buying jam. At a grocery store, she ran two tables promoting jam. The table with 24 types of jam tasters resulted in 3% of the people tasting buying a pot of jam. The table with six jams resulted in a huge 30% purchasing a jar of jam—fewer choices results in better engagement with the issue at hand.

It is a bit of a balancing act between not succumbing to a comfort zone where change is the big bad and varying life enough to keep things fresh and interesting without being overwhelming.

Some ways to manage the number of choices you need to take to avoid neural overwhelm and possible bad decisions include:

- Plan ahead. Meal plans, weekly to-dos, annual medicals, and vet visits can all be scheduled to happen up front, which reduces the decisions needed in the moment. You can even plan when you do your planning. I like to plan my week on a Sunday morning and clump all my annual stuff into November. Fewer choices to make right there.
- If you find a great product or service, note it down and make that your go-to. Occasionally, when you have the space in your life, you can try something new to keep things fresh and exciting.
- Keep items in logical, set places. For example, where important things like keys and your wallet go when you aren't using them or where items are stored in the bathroom, medicine cabinet, and kitchen.
- Have routines for activities that occur daily. It does not need to be time-related for them to occur in the same order. For example, you know that at night the kids need to do homework, have dinner, do chores, have some playtime, bathe, and have a bedtime routine. Deciding the order in which these things happen makes everything easier for you and them.
- Get rid of too many choices. Create a mix-and-match wardrobe or do what Steve Jobs did and wear only black jeans and turtlenecks. Simple things like food, clothes, products, and so on can be limited to a few things or one type of thing to make daily life easier. Remove temptation if needed. If you need to decide whether or not to have that glass of wine every evening and your willpower is weak by then, so you end up giving in, but your health is suffering, not keeping wine in the house is probably a good idea.
- Take the choice out of your own hands. Choose in advance and then commit by signing up, investing

money, or involving others who will require you to fulfill the initial commitment. This means that you don't need to keep deciding. It is clear there is more value in doing the thing than not.
- Reserve the start of the day for important decisions and put off big decisions until the following day if you can. When your brain is freshest, you have the most willpower and can make better decisions.

When you start feeling overwhelmed by life, one of the first places to look is at the number of choices you must make every day, and then look at ways to reduce and simplify this amount.

FOCUS

An immense complexity is the sheer amount of information and input we expose ourselves to daily. Our minds jump about like crazed monkeys from thought to thought, idea to idea. These monkey minds are encouraged to jump all over by the lives we lead. Constant checking of instant messages, missed calls, social media, and the internet teaches us an advanced level of distraction. There are few boundaries, and people can contact you whenever and wherever you are, and they do if you allow it.

We are told we need to focus, but we are not often taught how. And we definitely don't practice the skill much.

Our minds like to dwell in the past, ruminating about past hurts, mistakes, or problems more often than good memories. That leaves us feeling angry, resentful, guilty, or sad. When we aren't reliving an unhappy past (and by that, I do mean reliving, as each time you go there, your body responds as if that thing was happening again), we are letting our monkey minds race into an unknown and worrying future. This kind of unpleasant dwelling is where a lot of anxiety comes from. We fear the unknown because our imaginations run wild, but we often don't define what we are worried about. In this case, pretty much anything could happen to our minds, so we have a lot of hazy things to worry about. They build up and linger there, adding to our growing stress levels.

In reality, much of what we worry about does not happen or happens differently from how we pictured it. Again, our subconscious mind does not know the difference between reality and what we visualize, so it reacts much the same as if everything we are angsting about was happening right now. This worrying sets off the stress response, and we feel bad. To be honest, this is a little crazy because between the past and future; we sit in some permanent haze of bad feelings. If we pull our heads out of memories or future concerns and bring ourselves firmly but gently into the present moment, we will find that suddenly life becomes richer, calmer, and more joyful.

In each moment, there is so much peace to be found. It is at this moment that our actual life is unfolding. Each moment is adding to each moment. It is in these moments that our life exists. We will miss it if we don't learn to pull ourselves and our focus into the now.

Also, as a means of destressing, bringing your awareness into the present moment is generally very calming. Unless Godzilla is busy smashing our buildings, an impending tidal wave, or our kid has just run into a busy road, we will find that the present moment is pretty problem-free. So, in essence, we can fight or flee (take emergency action), which at that moment does not leave you feeling bad in any case, or we can enjoy the peace.

That sounds pretty good, right? So how do we do this?

First, handle outstanding past and future business. In the present time, the past serves as a learning tool. What lessons can you take and apply in your life now and going forward?

STRESS AND HOW TO MANAGE IT

For future concerns, spend some time writing them out.

What is on your mind or worrying you? Of these things, what is very likely to happen? What would be cataclysmic if it did happen? Those are the things you put your attention into first, then the cataclysmic–but not so likely, and then the less impactful stuff. Lastly, you can either deal with or mentally discard the unimportant and improbable stuff. I mean, aliens could land and steal your prize pooch, but it is not that likely. And if that happened, you may be sad, but it would be way more serious for the dog than you.

Once you have prioritized your worries, pop the likely ones into a list. Next to each fear or concern, write what could happen if this event occurred. Then next to that, write out what possible steps you could take to reduce the fallout or avoid it altogether.

For the less serious stuff that does need doing anyway, just put together some simple plans. Write it out for an easy later reference. What is the goal? Be specific. What steps will be needed? What resources or people will be needed? What are your time frames? How will you know when it is done correctly?

There are many apps and software programs that you can use and refer to once a day or week to make sure you have done what is needed in that time period. Honestly, I get by adequately with an online calendar (the Google calendar together with my client bookings on Facebook's appointment function works just fine) and my excel spreadsheets for more significant projects.

Once you have done this work, you can put all your plans and lists to one side and bring your attention back into the present moment, safe and secure in the knowledge that business has been handled.

Another part of managing your focus is simply being mindful of what movie your mind is playing. Just like watching a scary movie, or a comedy, what you are 'watching' will generate certain feelings. Even if you logically know that you are sitting on a couch watching

TV, your subconscious still reacts as if the thing was actually happening. That's why you can get scared in a horror movie, or inspired in a movie of hope and motivation.

What you are seeing in your mind's eye is much like this.

Allowing your focus to dwell on unhappy memories, fears, and suchlike is going to make you feel bad. Mindfully directing your focus onto what can or needs to be done now or onto happier memories or thoughts will energize and strengthen you. You have the choice; you really do. All it takes is an awareness of where your focus is going and also what is helpful to focus on and what is not.

DISTRACTIONS

There is a lot of 'noise' in our lives. Our phone rings and pings. Instant messages flood in. Constant ads, spam calls, and news snippets crowd our attention. This will never stop unless you stop it. You need to put the systems and boundaries in place and let others know what they are if necessary.

And that multi-tasking thing? Well, that's a bit of a joke. You will always find some wiseacre who insists they can multitask with ease. I laugh quietly (in my head so as not to be rude). The brain simply cannot and does not work that way. Each time you switch to a new activity (or context), it takes at least a few seconds to repurpose your brain in the different requirements of a separate task. Every time you are interrupted (or switch tasks), it can take up to half an hour to get back on track, losing a lot of time, and often means that none of the tasks are getting your full attention. This has to and does impact productivity and quality of work. Believe me, I can attest to this. As I write this, I have a teenager, five chickens, three cats, and some neighbors all vying for my attention, and it is taking five times as long to do as a result.

In summary, studies show that you lose an average of forty

percent of your productive time for two tasks, with 20% of your time lost to context switches.

Twenty percent of your productive time is spent on each task if you're multitasking three or more activities, and then you lose at least 40% of your time to context switching (Mackay, 2021).

Even Superman, who can probably multitask super fast, would lose a few minutes every day and probably drop a few screaming women (oops) in the process of multitasking.

Lastly, where you choose to put your focus has a significant impact on your mood. You can easily lose yourself in a blue funk or depression if you put your focus on a bunch of unhelpful, unhappy memories or thoughts. So learn to be selective about where you let that monkey mind go. Don't let it wreak destruction. Contain, direct and distract the monkey. You are in control, and you decide where you want your focus to go.

To improve your focus, you can use various exercises which strengthen your mental focus muscles. Things like daily meditation, sensory focusing exercises, and keeping yourself on task for a minimum of half an hour at a stretch all help train your brain to focus better. If you know that your cellphone or the internet is a big distraction, turn the phone off (with emergency calls allowed only), and put it in another room if you have to. Turn the internet off at the router if you can. Physically remove distractions just as you would if you were doing so for a busy toddler. If you can stick it out for a while, you will get more into the habit of focus and less into the habit of distraction.

GET CLEAR ON WHAT'S IMPORTANT

If you don't know what is truly important to you, it can be hard to understand how to simplify your life so that you remain satisfied and fulfilled by what is left.

This understanding is essentially the basis of your self-identity.

If something is not important to you, and you are forcing yourself, or being forced into it, you will feel resentful, frustrated, and irritable. People will, in the end, do what is important to them with more enjoyment and drive, than they will do other stuff. What is important to us also links to personal values. This is not something we often think about, but to clarify our purpose and life's meaning for us, we really should do this at least once or twice in our lifetimes.

We do change, so I prefer to do a more regular check-in. A really easy way to do it is to ask yourself, "What do I want?"

And then feel into the answer. Do you feel resistance or joy, fear or love, excitement or boredom? That will tell you very clearly and quickly if something is aligned with who you are or not.

Another way to know what is important to you is to look at your daily choices. These will give you a fair bit of insight. If you choose to spend hours watching a series, then rest and easy amusement may be more of a value than getting that book written, for example. If reading a bedtime story every night to your kids has to happen, this indicates that your children's wellbeing, education, and a sense of connection to them is a value. If you check the news and spend a few minutes every day reading up on new or interesting topics, perhaps knowledge is of value.

See what your choices tell you, about yourself and don't second-guess this. Don't try to impose a fantasy of who you would like to be over what is going on. By being completely honest with yourself, you will get a helpful awareness of who you are right now. This does not mean you can't change, improve, replace bad habits, and so on, just that you have a clear view of where you are at right now. This helps you know what needs to happen if change is on the cards.

Spend some time researching lists of values. Bravery, courage, connection, relationships, fun, peace, learning, honesty, survival, health, being proactive, loving, caring, helpful, or kind are all

STRESS AND HOW TO MANAGE IT

examples of values. Of course, there are many more. Do the work to identify what yours are.

Once you are more transparent on this, look at your life to see where what you are doing (or required to do) is not lined up with your values. For example, working for one organization left me stressed and almost permanently demotivated. When I Looked into it, I realized their values were money and success, and mine were honesty and humanity. Once I left that values clash behind me, my stress levels dropped significantly.

CREATE BOUNDARIES AND MAINTAIN THEM

For many years, a good friend has struggled with a rather narcissistic mother with whom she shares a home. In a moment of clarity, she shared with me that it had taken her so long to realize that boundaries are not about people respecting you so much as you putting limits in place and keeping them there.

Other people will not put boundaries in place for you. In fact, even when you put your own in place, they may not understand or respect those boundaries. Everyone is different, so you can't expect them all to understand your boundaries or why your boundaries exist.

They don't have to. They just need to know your boundaries and respect them after that. This means respecting your wishes in that regard. Do you even know what your boundaries are? Let's take a look.

Practical Exercise: Setting Boundaries

What do you like?
What don't you like?
What drives you wild, enrages you, or upsets you?
Think about a range of situations, people you know, and times

when you have felt a strong resistance, resentment, anger, or frustration. These feelings are an indication that you didn't like what was going on. Why? What value of yours does that link to, and what would you rather have happened? This applies mainly to your immediate person, home, and workspace. It definitely applies to anyone wanting to come into your space and interact with you on any level. You cannot impose your own values and boundaries on unrelated people and situations that do not touch on your life, as this would mean you are likely crossing their boundaries and being a controlling bully yourself. So yes, some stuff is not for you to control, and you need to know what these limits are.

Protection of the innocent and not causing harm to others are firm values for me. For example, I cannot watch someone being verbally or physically abusive to animals or children. My hackles go up, and I will step in and do something. I have been known to stop people in the street on this and require out-of-control parents to take a time out or get help if this stuff plays out in my sphere of influence. I cannot control every abusive person out there, but if I know of abuse, I am legally encouraged to report it and will. Abuse is not okay; it goes against the universal value of not harming others. I will also not tolerate anyone behaving in an abusive way towards me either.

However, another less crucial boundary is that I don't like people eating off my plate. I have shared this with my family, and they don't do it out of respect for me. If anyone else does this, I will tell them. If they do it again, I will not eat with them again. It is reasonably straightforward. When I see an errant hand straying for my plate, I am not above gently moving it away.

So make a list of these things you do not like or agree with. Link it to your values where you can and get clear on exactly what you will or will not tolerate.

Next, consider what actions you need to take to create, support, and defend this boundary.

A good place to start is communicating your preferences to whoever is concerned. Make sure they understand what it is you want and also why. They then have a chance to agree or not. If they disagree, that means they don't get to spend time with you. The end! This can equally apply to people who live with you. If you can't avoid or remove them, there are ways not to engage, walk away from and give no attention to bad behavior that infringes your space.

Saying no is hard for some people. You may need to practice this a bit in the mirror, on your own, at first. Then move up to smaller nos, and build up your confidence for the bigger ones. Keep going, and it will start feeling easier and more comfortable to do. And you don't need to explain your no. Just a polite no thank you is enough. Pair it with an enigmatic smile to add to the mystery if you want to.

People who don't respect your no, are not good for your soul. It is best to cut people like that out of your life as far as possible. Lack of respect for another's boundaries shows a level of selfishness, lack of empathy or care, and likely a bunch of other bullying or abusive behavior that will go with that. It is certainly not good to be around.

Next Steps

These are all vital steps to simplifying your life. As you start applying them, you will begin to breathe easier.

Keep in mind that just because a thing is physically possible does not mean it is psychologically wise. Consider where your real-life rewards lie and let that influence your decisions and actions.

Don't let others overload you with their own agendas and expectations that you haven't agreed to. Let them do them, and you do you. You don't need to trade your sanity and mental health for your to-do lists. It is just not worth it.

4

RELEASING STRESS

"Laughter is the valve on the pressure cooker of life. Either you laugh and suffer, or you got your beans...on the ceiling " - Wavy Gravy.

Well, no one wants beans on the ceiling. They are incredibly hard to clean off.

Speaking of ceilings, there was once a pancake that stayed stuck to my grandma's kitchen ceiling for about two months. Every day the excitement mounted. Would today be the day the pancake dropped? All the kids had to walk under the pancake at least once a day, resulting in laughter and shrieks. My one cousin, who was only five, would cry and cry when it was her turn to walk under the pancake—poor little Jenny. And oh, the pressure! When it eventually detached itself and fell on grandpa, we all had a good laugh. Jenny was so relieved too.

Life is full of pancakes about to drop. They come in the form of bills, deadlines, looming holidays, projects, health, relationships, and more. You can either let them hang over you like the pancake of Damocles, and cry and stress about it, or you can find ways to release the tension.

Just like stress and pressure build from a lot of smaller things, until we feel like we may explode, we can take small steps to reduce and release this pressure. There is no one-off solution. Stress release consists of a bunch of actions you can take regularly. Over and above managing your mindset and physical health, we have many options.

Because of our brain-body connection, we can work either from the brain and thus calm the body or from the physical, thus calming the brain and mind.

JOURNALING

Journaling is best done by hand. Writing engages your brain on a very different, more analytical level than typing on a keyboard.

I like to use a lovely notebook or hand-crafted, covered journal. Using a special pen or pencil and sitting quietly on my shady porch enjoying the garden or at my study desk in the quiet evening makes the whole process special and enjoyable.

Journaling regularly, either daily or once a week, is a great way to reflect on your life and organize your thoughts. It helps bring your awareness onto your thoughts, which is where it needs to be if you are going to manage thought patterns and sift any unhelpful ones out of the mix.

While writing, you can clarify problems, worries, and fears and identify any negative inner talk.

There are many ways to journal, and you can even run more than one, depending on their purpose. A self-reflective journal can be a collection of free-flowing thoughts, drawings, pressed flowers, and photos. It can have a specific intention too. A journal can track mood, physical, and mental elements. It could be a gratitude or success journal that lists things you are grateful for or have done well on that day. This kind of journaling is a great way to focus on positive and uplifting stuff right before bed or to set the tone at the beginning of the day.

Keep your journal somewhere safe. Your journal is a safe space where you can vent and release your most private thoughts and feelings, so it is not for anyone else to read unless you wish them to.

MUSIC THERAPY

If you've ever cranked up your music while driving or after a rough day, you will know how marvelously your favorite tunes can soothe a ruffled soul. Whether it is hard rock, metal, Bach, or some chilled out reggae hardly seems to matter if it works to release the stress build-up from your day.

Music has a profound effect on emotions. Speed the music up and your heart rate increases, and you feel energized, slow it down and feel physically and mentally calmer.

People who have experienced brain trauma, such as a stroke, or who have speech disorders are able to communicate with singing when their brain remains unable to reproduce the spoken word. Singing, sounds, and music operates on a whole different neural level to other forms of communication, and engages more with those parts of the brain involved with emotion, memory, focus, and emotion processing (Gupta, 2012).

Sound therapy is increasingly understood as tangible therapy. Sound at about 60 beats per minute causes the brain to synchronize with the tempo, generating alpha brain waves that are good for focus, calm and learning, a meditative state triggered by sound. Delta brainwaves induced by around five hertz (sound cycles per second) help you fall asleep.

Music that is proven to relieve stress includes string instruments, flutes, and drums, like you find in Native American, Indian, and Celtic music. Nature sounds such as running water, the sound of waves and the sea, rain, forest sounds, and so on are all very calming.

Another interesting application of sound healing is the use of solfeggio frequencies. Many people use MHz healing as one of the easiest ways to access the brain via the body, circumventing our conscious mind and working directly on the required areas of healing. Youtube has a stack available for free:

174 Hz relieves pain, inflammation, and stress.

285 Hz heals cells, tissues, and organs.

304 normalizes blood pressure.

396 Hz releases fear and guilt.

417 Hz removes negative energy in and around you.

432 Hz helps you focus.

528 Hz is great for personal transformation and DNA repair.

639 Hz reconnects you with your relationships and with love and peace.

741 Hz encourages self-expression and helps you find solutions.

852 Hz brings you reconnection spiritually.

963 HZ creates room for oneness and unity. It is known as "the frequency of the Gods".

999 HZ provides divine protection.

Choose one at bedtime, and put it on a timer, so it stops playing after a few hours. I use this method often and always wake up refreshed and feeling a lot better the next day. Another way to access MHz is with the use of Tibetan singing bowls, although it is hard to reproduce a specific MHz this way as an amateur.

Whether these MHz are a placebo effect or not, the proof for me is in the healing. Creating a sound bath of your chosen sounds and frequencies means that you can release stress, quickly generate a sense of calm and energy and that all means that ultimately you will be functioning better all around.

Music has a direct, proven impact on the entire psychobiological system and in calming the normal stress fight-or-flight response, the endocrine and nervous systems. Even music played before a stressful event can positively affect how resilient you are when things happen (Thoma et al. 2013). With such a powerful destressing tool so easily and readily available, it is a no-brainer to work it in more regularly for a calmer life.

Create a few upbeat and calming playlists. Listen to them while driving or commuting, when doing chores, and even at work if you have headphones and can get away with it. Use music to calm yourself and your family. I have effectively used it over the years in all of these ways and even to calm a child going through a challenging life stage. We played a "happy" playlist every day on the way to school and sang along. He was a better-behaved child on those days, and on the days we missed or forgot, his teachers would invariably ask me what had happened as he was acting out way more than usual. It was almost too predictable.

Honestly, even my plants grow better, except when I play heavy metal. Apparently, even plants are music critics, sigh!

Some soundtracks to try out include:

Weightless by Marconi Union, which is said to be one of the most relaxing soundtracks written.

What a Wonderful World by Louis Armstrong.

Let It Be by The Beatles.

Your Song by Elton John and Bernie Taupin.

Watermark by Enya.

And *Canzonetta Sull'aria* by Mozart.

You are not limited to what other people like. There are so many fabulous soundtracks and artists to choose from. If the music is relaxing for you, that is all that matters in the end.

AROMATHERAPY

On a different sensory level altogether, we find yet another clever method to directly access our brain via our body, and that is our sense of smell.

Studies using aromatherapy show a significant reduction in stress when using aroma treatments (Seo, 2006). The Harvard Brain Science Initiative shows how smell, memory, and mood are all closely linked. Odors directly access the limbic part of the brain, as well as the amygdala and hippocampus, and all of these are related to emotions and memories.

That is probably why the smell of baking will take you back to the warm confines of grandma's kitchen, leaving you with happy memories and good feelings. Cinnamon, spices, citrus, and the smell of snow and evergreens take many of us back to Christmas and holiday memories. Think of what other smells you know are linked to happy memories for you, as this is a powerful way to feel better quickly.

"When you are walking down the street, consciously indicate what you are smelling ... the more you use [your nose], the stronger it gets." — Dawn Goldworm.

Using smell as part of sensory exercises is a good way to improve focus and mindfulness. In fact, a large part of tastes and flavors have to do with your ability to smell. Remove that, and often people cannot identify what it is they are eating.

The emotions and memories related to certain scents are used by home resellers, hotels, advertising aficionados, and more. Olfactory "branding" is becoming quite a thing as more people wise up to the importance of smell. Not to mention that we are attracted to potential life partners and mates via our olfactory sense of their pheromones.

With aromatherapy, you can do more than access your olfactory senses. Because aroma oils are made from concentrated plant oils, each of which has various effects on the body, you can inhale healing. Stimulating the immune system, clearing congestion and reducing inflammation, regulating blood pressure, and easing muscle tension are all possible with the right aromatherapy oils.

Find yourself an aromatherapy diffuser, burner, and a few oils to blend as needed. Most oils are not safe to ingest and are for topical use or inhalation only. Oils can be added to showers, baths or sprinkled on pillows or linens to be effective. About 15 to 20 drops of the oil in a bath works fine. If you are going to use oils more extensively, be sure to check dilution guidelines. Homemade lotions and creams are fun to blend for yourself. About 10 to 15 drops of your active oil per 125 ml of base/carrier oil or lotion (like aqueous cream or coconut oil) is a safe dilution for adults. You can use aroma oils in a necklace diffuser or as a perfume so that you can experience the healing and calming effect all through the day. For your own room spray, mix 30 to 40 drops of your chosen oil or blend of oils into 50 ml vodka, 50 ml water, and add a tablespoon of salt. Shake and spray as needed.

There are hundreds of uses and interesting blends, and recipes for aromatherapy products online. So if this interests you, you can take this learning a lot further.

Just be careful as if you have small children or pets, check that the oils you are using are safe for them first. We tend to think that it will not affect us that much because it is being inhaled, but in reality, it does. So practice care with this tool.

The top choices for destressing include lavender, rose, bergamot, chamomile, clary sage, sandalwood, and ylang-ylang. To lift your mood, try rosemary, lemon, or jasmine. Try blends with lavender, ylang-ylang, and chamomile to sleep deeply. Orange and rosemary are more energizing and helpful when you need to focus and remember, like when studying. Sandalwood and lavender are particularly good for calming anxiety and panic. Play around and blend various oils until you find a blend that works for you.

CRYOTHERAPY

Dutch motivational speaker Wim Hof is well known for his support of this method. Known as the "iceman," he takes daily long swims in the icy water of Poland and promotes his cold water therapy approach with breathing techniques that many swear have revolutionized their lives.

Cold water therapy, also known as cryotherapy, helps reset the nervous system and brain and has been shown to have a direct impact on neural messaging as well as helping reduce inflammation in the body and brain. This helps manage pain levels and calms a stressed-out or depressed state.

Ice baths have been used for mental and physical health purposes for thousands of years. The age-old sweat lodge or sauna was generally paired with immersing oneself in cold water as well.

Professional athletes use it to ease inflamed muscles and recover physically all around. The cold helps constrict blood vessels and open back up afterward, which helps your body flush out toxins and oxygenate the entire system. Cold temperatures are also great for weight loss. It activates brown fat tissue, using stored fat reserves to help you warm up. On a neurological level, over and above reducing inflammation, it stimulates the vagus nerve and increases the parasympathetic nervous system, which is all about rest, digestion, and a calm state. This, in turn, reduces stress levels and also helps with gut health.

Start with a few minutes of cold water at the end of your shower. After a few weeks, you can slowly increase the time spent under the cold water vs. warm water. You become more used to the colder temperature and even withstand the whole shower using cold water. I would not recommend graduating to ice baths without first getting a medical check-up and getting an ice bath expert to be there while you are trying this out. If you have any heart problems, there is a risk of tachycardia or arrhythmia. Hypothermia and shock are also possibilities, so always do this in a responsible and controlled fashion, with help on hand. The idea is to gradually increase exposure to cold water therapy and not rush it too quickly.

NATURE BATHS

Immersing yourself in the smells, sight, and sounds of a forest, field, or beach is so immediately calming and soothing to your senses that it is one of the best ways to destress on a regular basis.

Even if you live in a city, see if you can find a local park, away from the traffic, rush, and noise. Regular trips into the countryside are invaluable to keep your mood lifted and stress at bay.

Some of us are luckier, and have access to lovely garden spaces, and live close to all the delights and beauty of nature. Even then, we can take this bounty for granted or seldom take the time to enjoy it. The average person spends 93% of their time indoors, in the office or house (Li, 2018), so we lose out on a readily available stress release option.

The Japanese have turned the art of forest bathing, or shinrin-yoku, into a much-needed therapy for those who live in large, crowded cities. Being amongst nature and connecting to it with all one's senses is proven to lower blood pressure, heal the nervous system, improve immune response, and reduce anxiety and stress.

The comfort and ease we feel, plus the sensory chill factor, all add up to a relaxing experience, no matter how citified you may be.

To make the most of a nature destress session:

- Find a spot somewhere green or natural.
- Put all devices away (and off) and resist the temptation to reach for them, even to take photographs.
- Slowly meander with no specific purpose.
- Let nature seep in via all your senses. You can use this time to meditate, pray, do some yoga, write with pencil and paper, hug a tree, get some light exercise walking (which doubles the stress release factor), or even take your paints, brushes, and a blank canvas and spend the time painting what you see.

There does not need to be an agenda, timeframe, or goal. Simply be in the moment and absorb the peace.

MOVEMENT

We have already spoken about how important any form of physical activity is for mood management. A few minutes every day, or 20 to 30 minutes a few times a week of any fairly brisk activity of your choice, will quickly start showing great results.

Apart from working stress chemicals out of your system faster, it also increases physical resilience, improves digestion, circulation, blood pressure, sleep, strength and endurance. All of these things have a direct impact on maintaining a good mood.

Whatever you choose to do, make sure it does not further complicate your life and add to your neverending to-do list. Make it something that makes sense for you, and matches your interests, and physical abilities.

Aerobic exercise boosts your heart rate, releases endorphins, and works off stress hormones fast. Some of the best ways to quickly activate these benefits, especially right after a stressful event, include brisk walks, a quick jog or run, cycling, swimming, or just putting on your favorite tune and dancing the stress off in the privacy of your living room.

If you have the time and money, joining a HIIT class, boxing, kickboxing, and many of the martial arts are also focused ways to channel excess stress-energy safely.

AFFIRMATIONS & VISUALIZATIONS

One way to lift your spirits is to have a couple of inspiring goals for your life. When we have meaning and a purpose, it energizes everything. Any stress experienced in this state is more of a positive, motivating kind of stress.

You have already defined your values, aka what is important to you. Have you got some idea of what direction you could pick that might align with that? For example, if a value is an education, perhaps a life goal might be obtaining certification or a qualification in your field of interest. Perhaps your values include family and relationships, and a goal is quality time with your partner and children.

Take some time to remind yourself of what you want for your life. What do you want your days to look and be like? What would you like to achieve in the next year? Where do you want to live? Who do you want to be spending time with? What quality of life do you want?

Shortlist your dreams and desires.

Now write them into short affirmations. This technique needs to be in a specific formula for them to access your subconscious and work effectively.

Affirmations need to state very clearly and specifically what it is you want. They need to be written in the present tense as if they are already happening. Speaking directly to your subconscious mind in such a way that it convinces it that if the thing has already happened, it is more likely to happen again. That means it builds belief in the possibility of the desired situation. Lastly, it helps to use emotions in the mix. Picture how you will feel when what you want has happened (or is happening). Add that into the sentence.

For example:

"I am completing my first year of business studies, and I feel motivated."

"I am enjoying a relaxing holiday at the beach with my children."

"I am peaceful living in my new home in the country."

"I am handling difficult moments calmly and feel increasingly calm and peaceful."

Working your destress goals in is probably a good idea.

Make about four or five of these short affirmations. You need to keep it focussed on priorities and not overwhelm your mind with too many. Put them on a list that you can read aloud first thing in the morning and last thing at night. Stick them somewhere you will see all the time.

You can even take them and combine them with visuals, images, color pictures, and create a vision board collage that you can stick up as a constant visual. This is another clever way to access your subconscious mind and reinforce the likelihood of these things happening.

Write your wishes into a visualization if you want to level up this whole idea. Do it scene by scene, and make it very descriptive, using all the senses you can. This all helps it feel more real. You can read it back to yourself or record it and play it back at least five or six times to plant it firmly in your mind.

All of these steps will make achieving your goals a lot easier from a confidence and personal motivation point of view at the very least. You still need to also take the necessary steps that move you closer to your goals. Affirmations simply make this more tangible and easily achievable.

Once you achieve your goals, make new affirmations and rinse and repeat. It might seem a little strange at first, but the science of how our subconscious mind works supports the efficacy of this tool. You will soon start seeing progress towards the kind of life you want if done right.

MEDITATION

I hear so many people say that they can't meditate or that it is too difficult. They can't focus, their mind wanders, and thinking of nothing is not possible. This means they don't understand what meditation really is all about or how simple it can be.

Once you have tried it out for a few days in a row, meditation starts becoming self-reinforcing. The extreme relaxation and calm you begin to feel means that the more you do it, the more you will want to do it.

The practice of meditation helps strengthen your focus mental muscles, reduces stress levels, and helps regulate mood. Research has even linked it to more stable blood pressure, improved immune system, and reduced pain levels.

It is all about calm and focus. As it strengthens, this ability means you can be less reactive, and more productive on every level in your life. It has even been shown to increase neural connections and thicken the brain's prefrontal cortex, which is the bit involved with concentration, decision making, and increased awareness. It increases serotonin, and endorphins decreases stress chemicals, and increases DHEA (a longevity hormone) (Ask the Scientists, 2021).

The easiest way to meditate is the basic breathing-and-counting technique taught by Buddhists:

- Set your phone on a timer for a few minutes only. What short period of time do you feel the least resistance to? Pick that at first. Once the habit is more set, you can increase your meditation time later.
- Find a spot and a time of day when you will not be interrupted.
- Get comfortable. There is no specific way you need to sit. You can even lie down if you want.
- Keep your eyes open. Life does not happen with your eyes closed, and you want to get used to dropping into the meditative state of focussed calm whenever and wherever you are.
- Now, breathe slowly and deeply, and count your breaths. If thoughts intrude, gently bring your attention back onto counting. Start again from one if you have lost your place.
- Stop when your timer goes off.

After a few days of this, you should start noticing a definite difference in your overall ability to focus and feel calmer.

PLAY AND LAUGHTER

No matter how serious things get, laughter needs to be part of life. Unless hugely inappropriate, laughter eases tension, relaxes everyone who hears it and lifts the spirits. A well-placed joke creates a bridge between you and your audience and creates a sense of trust, relatability, and connection.

The short-term effect of a good laugh stimulates your internal organs, activates and relieves your stress response, stimulates circulation, and relaxes your muscles. Long-term, it encourages a better mood by lifting your spirits, promoting a healthy immune system, reducing pain by producing endorphins, and improving self-esteem.

Laughter does not come easy to everyone, but there are ways to work it into your life more often.

- Hang around funny, happy people.
- Watch funny videos online. With Youtube, Tik Tok, and all the many prolific channels providing free content, you are bound to find something that appeals to your sense of humor.
- Watch TV/movie comedies or stand-up comedy shows.
- Find humorous podcasts to listen to.

Just make sure that your fun isn't at the expense or in any way harmful to others.

CONNECTION

Humans are not meant to be alone. We are social. We feel fear and insecurity when we are cut off from the safety of the group. This is programmed into us.

A sense of connection is vital for our mental health. This does not always have to mean a connection to other people. It can be a connection to ourselves through greater self-awareness, connection to nature and mother earth, or an idea.

The social side is recommended, though. It is not that people will provide all the answers or solve any incompletion within you. What they do is reflect and provide opportunities to learn. Depending on the relationship, they provide solace and company and sometimes even need support. If you aren't a very sociable person, you don't need to attend a bunch of parties. A few quality relationships with people you can feel comfortable, or inspired by, are fine.

People can be helpful. They can share knowledge and resources, and more brains and hands mean more can be achieved. From a neural point of view, interacting with others stimulates neurogenesis and memory. These are all good reasons to reach out and develop strong relationships where you can.

If you are going through a period where you feel disconnected in general, look at ways to reconnect with life. Nature walks, joining groups online or face-to-face, getting out to attend interesting talks and events, or even just getting a pet for company and to cuddle are all ways you can start reconnecting and feeling better.

5

HAVING A STRESSLESS LIFE

"If each day is a gift, I would love to know where I can return my Mondays."
- John Wagner.

When in the first flush of youth, life challenges are more exciting for many. Life is still new and interesting. Then the rat race, bills, and the humdrum cycle of work, home, chores, eat, sleep, work sets in. Most people in their late twenties and thirties begin to feel mounting pressure. The demands of a growing family have their own stress load for those who have chosen to have children. Life is busy and demanding, and even worse, often a little meaningless, which adds to these feelings of stress. The good news is that at some point, growth and learning happen. With time comes a certain maturity, and with that may also come a greater feeling of fulfillment and inner peace.

Looking back at my own life, I realize that I had to learn some things for myself. But I also know that if I could have understood some key concepts about time, workload, other people, and myself, I could have stressed a lot less and had a much better journey.

Understanding these things will mean that you can manage

your stress levels earlier and reduce the chances of burnout or breakdown.

A lot of it has got to do with your outlook and perspective.

FRUSTRATION

At the root of much of our stress is a certain level of frustration. Things aren't going the way we want them to. Maybe the events are not what we wanted or expected. There are delays, extra workloads, and difficult people to deal with. Perhaps you are running late, the kids are acting up, or that business deal fell through.

At its heart, frustration is the inner resistance to what is happening. There is the thought that *it should not be this way*. That creates inner tension as you compare what it is to what you expected or wanted and find the new situation lacking. This tension builds up and erupts out of you in some form of irritation or even anger. You may try to force things to go the way you originally wanted or just seethe with bad feelings due to that thought you just had.

Notice, we are not referring to the situation but your thoughts about it.

One of the inevitable parts of life is change. There is no life without challenges, truly. So understanding and accepting that no matter how well you plan, there will be surprises or variations at times is the first step to finding that inner calm.

It is what it is. Here you sit, in this moment, where whatever it is is happening. Unless you have a time machine, you cannot go back and change or fix it, nor can you fast forward out of this mess. Assuming that it is a mess, of course.

What is actually happening by allowing yourself to go down the rabbit hole of frustration?

Well, you are thinking about what you are not getting or doing, you are thinking about shoulds and should nots, and also that this is not fair, or desired, or whatever other negative thoughts you are now having. This creates a range of horrible emotions and takes up your focus and energy.

In the time that you sit in frustration, are you being productive? Are you doing something useful or helpful to you? Are you feeling good?

No?

What then is the point of spending valuable time in this sorry state?

The trick is to catch yourself in this reactive state and dial it all down. Let go of the unhelpful thoughts about what is happening and engage with what is happening itself. Is this situation entirely bad? Can you find some good in it? Is there anything you can do to improve things? Is there something else you can do instead? Instead of these negative thoughts that make you reactive, is there something else you can think about instead of these negative thoughts?

For example, you get stuck in traffic while driving into an important meeting. The traffic is standing still, and there is nothing anyone can do at this moment. You can get all reactive, honk your horn, smack the steering wheel in anger, and let off a bunch of expletives. This gets you even hotter and more frustrated, and when you eventually get to the meeting, you will not be in a state to be that friendly or productive. Your other option is to stop all the frustration. The traffic is the traffic. What can you do? Perhaps you can call the office and let them know you may be running late. Perhaps you can choose another route. Perhaps you can play an audiobook, or some of your favorite music, sit back in your seat, and put some effort into enjoying this brief respite. Perhaps you can people watch. Look at how everyone else is handling things. Look at the silly ones getting all heated up and the zen ones who return your smiles. After all, you cannot go anywhere right now; you may as well make the most of this quiet time. Your anger and frustration will certainly not remove all these vehicles in front of you magically. It is just going to make you feel bad—what a waste of energy.

Reframing your perspective on unforeseen events is the only logical way to proceed.

EMOTIONAL ATTACHMENT THEORY

When life doesn't go your way, there is that immediate, sharp pang of disappointment, isn't there? You wanted that thing so badly, and now it isn't happening. Perhaps something less pleasant is unfolding before your eyes. Oh no!

The degree to which you have invested your emotions into certain outcomes will decide how deeply you feel this disappointment and possible frustration. If you have attached a lot of emotions, you will feel pretty bad. If you attach a lot of emotions to most things in your life, you are going to feel bad a lot of the time.

This does not mean you never feel anything. What it does mean is that you need to be more mindful of where you choose to invest your emotional energy. You need to prioritize and evaluate whether a person, goal, or situation is worth this emotional spend and how much of it you will invest.

Try viewing this as a bank account, if that helps. Let's call this emotional currency eBucks, just for fun.

For example, say you are emotionally attached to your day going smoothly. You put some of your eBucks in the good-traffic account, some into the nice-boss account, the good-kids account, the delicious-dinner account, and the no-problems account. So you are pretty thinly spread. Then the traffic is rubbish, your boss is having a bad day, and so are your kids, you burn the dinner, and the troubles keep mounting.

Suddenly all those investments are not paying back, and now your emotional bank account is empty, and you are unhappy.

As an alternative, perhaps you have decided to only invest some of your precious eBucks into making some progress on a project that is close to your heart or into the hope that you will have quality time cuddling with your children before bed. Look, these things can still get derailed, but they are more controllable and specific. They are limited to one or two things that are truly important to you, and that means that you are not emotionally drained by anything else that happens or does not happen in your day.

Suppose you invest all your emotional resources into many everyday situations that stand a real chance of not playing out exactly as expected. In that case, you are soon going to run out of resources. This is plain bad investing; ask any investment banker.

If you take a more careful approach and only invest in something that aligns with your values or gives deeper meaning to your existence, you will still get something of value back, even if it does not work the way you envisioned. If you assess each situation and decide how much of yourself it warrants, you will not blow all your emotions on the small stuff. You will keep them for the truly pivotal things and assess what a good investment versus a not-so-sure one is.

Emotions are tools. They are messengers of mental and physical health and tell you when something is not right in your world or yourself. They are also tools that help you achieve goals. You can drive those goals more effectively by putting your eBucks into the stuff that matters for you. Attaching positive emotions to hopes and dreams that you also then plan, put some effort into is a great way to energize the entire undertaking.

But there is a little trick to this. When you visualize whatever it is you want, you allow yourself to feel the good feelings you would have if it happened in the way you want. You do the work in terms of plans, resources, time, and effort. And then, you let it go. You take those big emotions and lay them aside. You focus on other areas of your life once you have done what you can for this thing that you want. At this stage, by letting go, stepping back, and allowing the situation to unfold as it will, you remove the risk of feeling extremely bad if it does not all go according to plan.

Start becoming more aware also of where you are investing emotions. Consciously decide that you will not invest in things entirely outside of your control, are not unpredictable, or are not a priority. These unanticipated events and situations that will not be remembered or important a few hours from now, or a few days, are not worth investing any of your precious emotional energy into. This especially applies to random everyday stuff, like how others behave or the small day-to-day events that happen regardless.

Once you have made this conscious decision, you will find a large amount of frustration and anger disappears. When someone misbehaves or something in your day happens, that makes life a bit more difficult. You don't have that painful twinge anymore. You shrug and handle business calmly. You can do this because you are not emotionally invested in things beyond your control.

You are not a horrible person. It is not that you don't care about anyone or anything. You reserve your care for those truly important things. Knowing your values can be quite helpful, too, as you can shortlist what these are for you upfront. What you are, then, is a much calmer, emotionally stable person who is much nicer to be around too.

THE POWER OF WORDS AND STORIES

"When I look back on all these worries, I remember the story of the old man who said on his deathbed that he had had a lot of trouble in his life, most of which had never happened" - Winston Churchill.

The words you use about yourself and your life have incredible power over your frame of mind and have a knock-on effect on your feelings, actions, and overall mood.

Considering that words are based on a thought you need to have before you express yourself outwards, it comes back to that negative inner talk thing and your overall root beliefs about the world.

The same set of facts can be related in many ways. Some empower, leaving the speaker, listener, or reader feeling good, hopeful, and inspired. Other options can leave you feeling pretty drained and weakened, almost as if you are reliving the moment the words describe. Words can uplift or break down a soul. And yet not many people are mindful of how they use them.

When you become good at noticing the words and stories you and the people around you are using, you will even find that you get an instant insight into the speaker or writer. Look at how they speak about themselves and others, and about challenging situations, and then look at where they are and how happy and calm they are, and you will start seeing some clear links.

Let's look at an example.

"I had a terrible childhood. We never had any money, and I had to share dresses, toys, sweets, and bedrooms with my other siblings. I even had to wear a homemade outfit to school dances and felt so lame compared to the other kids in their jeans and brand-name stuff. Everything was a struggle, and when I graduated from high school, the only way I could get a further education was with heavy student loans that took me many years to pay back."

Okay, how did that passage make you feel? Good, happy, uplifted? No?

Let's take the same example, with the same set of facts, and tell this story a bit differently.

"We didn't have a lot growing up. But it was okay. We managed to get by, and by sharing stuff with each other, we all had enough. In fact, that brought me closer to my sibs. Although my parents didn't have a lot of money, we survived. My mom had learned how to sew and was good at it. She made me some designer, one-of-a-kind outfits that made me stand out at school dances. When everyone wore jeans and the same clothes, my outfits were special. Yes, it was hard at times, but I graduated and gained entry into some good colleges. Luckily I qualified for a student loan, and that way, I got my degree which has helped me get some well-paying jobs."

Do you see the difference?

It is not that the speaker has changed the base facts. They have taken another viewpoint, and chosen to describe their story differently and positively. You don't need to be blind to reality or reinvent a thing. Consider what the upsides and good things are or were. How else can this story of yours be told?

Practical Exercise: Write a New Story

This exercise has a lot to do with the power of both words and focus. Remember, where you put your attention is what is real for you at that moment.

Think back over your life. Write down some of the big events, turning points, and choices you made that left you feeling less than happy.

- Pick one or two of these stories, and extract the base facts. Remove all feelings, opinions, or anything that you can't verify.
- Now think about any good that may have come from this situation. Brainstorm this, and don't let your negative inner critic out for this part. It may just be a lesson you learned that helped prevent a similar thing from happening again to yourself or others.
- Rewrite your story with just the facts and a focus on the

positive side of the situation as far as you are able. Also, focus on how you became stronger, and how you made it through, and how this helps you now.

Not every story can be totally turned around, but it can be lightened and eased somewhat. Bear in mind that you are not doing this for anyone else. This is for you. This is to help you feel stronger, more at ease, more empowered, and confident.

WATCH OUT FOR THOUGHT TRAPS

Part of our mental make-up is specific very human thought tendencies. We have probably all fallen foul of them at some time or another. The thing is, when we are in the faulty thinking trap, we can't always see that we are. We can learn what to look out for, review past behavior in light of this, and be more mindful of not succumbing to it going forward.

Confirmation bias is one of the most common thought traps. This is where we filter new information and focus on only those parts that confirm what we think we already know. We discount or ignore anything that goes against what we have already decided. This means we cannot be genuinely open-minded or objective. Our viewpoint is skewed and unbalanced; we might not make the most informed or best choices as a result. For example, a wife has decided her husband is lazy. Anything he does to contribute to the home and workload is minimized or criticized, and she focuses only on those things he forgets to do, gets wrong, or does not do. How can he feel appreciated or valued in this situation? Inevitably he gives up trying, and it becomes a self-fulfilling prophecy.

False consensus is another insidious thought trap that has us assuming that everyone feels and thinks the same way we do. We don't realize how different others truly are, even those close to us. Even if we share common experiences and backgrounds, we cannot assume that others have the same root beliefs, world views, thoughts, and feelings as we do. It is just not possible. The extension of this thought trap is that when people make different choices than you would have, you judge them in light of what you would have done and often find them wanting. So when they turn down your idea, it becomes personal. Surely they should know better, and they are behaving this way on purpose to offend you or because there is something wrong with them. In fact, there is likely nothing wrong with them. They have different needs, values, views, likes, dislikes, and different boundaries. For example, your partner decides to spend their day off playing a computer game they just bought instead of helping you plant those new seedlings in the garden. Due to your false consensus thinking, you decide to take their behavior personally, as you assume that everyone (and especially them) should like gardening. You decide that they are avoiding you, aren't invested in the relationship, or keeping the home looking nice. Perhaps they are getting even with you for that time you didn't want to watch that boring car movie with them?

In reality, they want some downtime to do something of their own choice. They don't enjoy gardening and think the garden looks fine as it is. You have taken a perfectly normal and acceptable desire to spend spare time on a pastime of one's choice and made it wrong through the filter of how you see the world. Plants are your hobby, not theirs. But you extend your feelings about it onto them and then judge everything in light of that. Can you see how this can cause you some considerable stress?

The actor-observer bias is when we think that what we do is due to outside influences but that what other people do is due to internal choices and accountability. For example, when we run late for work, we quickly blame the traffic or cite whatever external factor made us late. When one of our colleagues is late, we may instead decide that they are lazy and irresponsible.

There are many more thought traps, like victim mentality,

STRESS AND HOW TO MANAGE IT

where everything that happens to you is someone else's fault, and you never take responsibility for your part. Negative bias is when you focus on only the bad bits of a situation and block out the good stuff.

These faulty thinking patterns can make life so much more difficult for you and others. They can lead to a bunch of unnecessary trouble, like communication breakdowns, escalating conflicts, and a lot of frustration.

How do you avoid falling into these thought traps? Well, it isn't easy, but observing your thoughts helps. Asking yourself how you know a thing is true, looking for counterevidence and being as open as possible to evaluate it, and asking lots of questions of yourself, your choices, and those of others. Getting a balanced set of facts as far as you are able is always a good start.

MINDING YOUR HABITS

A lot of the methods mentioned in this book require you to make some changes, perhaps. Whether these changes are to your diet, exercise routine, thought patterns, or behaviors, it will still take a little bit extra to get there.

First, some patience is needed when starting something new. The more you try to force and control, the more you may find that thing wriggle out of your grasp. So the first rule of change is to release your grip, be kind to yourself, and drop all-or-nothing thinking. This means that if you revert back to old ways momentarily, miss a day of the new habit (or two), or make a mistake, this does not mean it is the end of the world or that you have failed.

Every new skill or habit takes time to strengthen. You will make mistakes that are almost a given. What you are going for here is more of an average of the new choice over time. Go for "mostly," not "always." Begin again every day if you have to. Getting too hard on yourself and judgemental will only demotivate you and make this all so much more challenging to achieve. Even one less sugar rush is a plus for your body. One time that you show compassion to yourself or that you don't react angrily but rather respond calmly will make a difference. We build the new one piece at a time and celebrate each success, no matter how small.

Don't try to change too much all at once. Pick one thing at a time, and wait until you find that doing that thing is happening fairly effortlessly and without too much thought on your part. When that occurs, it means the new habit is fairly well set, and you can then move on to the next thing you wish to improve.

Make the first steps small once you have decided what you will be putting energy into. Choose to do (or be) this new thing in the smallest, simplest possible way. It must be a way that has you feeling the least resistance to the change. With most habits, this means doing the new activity for only a few minutes a day at first. Only once the habit is set will you add extra time or complexity. It is also best to choose an earlier time of day to start anything new, as you have less decision fatigue in the morning and so doing something unfamiliar is easier.

Sometimes you can bundle the new activity with an existing one, like combining your exercise with getting to work and back, for example. Walking or cycling to the office could replace that five-minute commute. Or bundle drinking more water with your hourly break. This also makes it easier and quicker.

The trick with habituating anything new is being as consistent as possible. Depending on what it is, practice it simultaneously, every day. Doing the same thing and using the same sequence of events are all recommended if you want this to habituate quicker.

The trigger and reward are pretty important too. With anything we habitually do, there will be a trigger, or what comes immediately before the habit. And also, there will be a reward for doing the thing. Knowing this, you can use it to replace old, unwanted habits and set new ones.

If you are replacing an unwanted habit, awareness of the trigger helps you alter it. Understanding of the habit itself and the corresponding reward is also useful. These are things that can be changed or used effectively with the new wanted behavior.

For example, say that you have the habit of losing your temper and raising your voice. You have enough self-awareness to see the damage this is doing to you and others, and you would like to change it. You can break it down like this:

- What is the unwanted habit? What will I replace it with, realistically? In our example, you don't want the shouting and losing self-control. You do want to stay calm, collected, and constructive. For this, you could look at counting and breathing to delay the emotional reaction or put yourself in a mental or physical time out for a few minutes. You could carry a smooth rock, or a stress ball, or wear a piece of jewelry to remind you and use it to refocus.
- What is the trigger? For the anger example, perhaps you identify that you are mainly triggered whenever people pressurize you with too many demands all at once. With anger, there is often more than one trigger and some underlying core beliefs and fears to deal with, but let's simplify for the purpose of this exercise.
- How could you alter the trigger? You could notice when it is happening and remove yourself. You could ask others to check in to see if it is a good time to make requests, or ask them to only ask you one thing at a time, or even to write it down what they need rather than do it verbally. What other options do you have? Brainstorm it, and involve any other role players in this trigger problem-solving.
- What is the reward? Well, quite often, someone who

lashes out in anger gets given a little more space. People stop and back off. Sometimes, you are forcing them to drop their demands or reduce them. Sadly the long-term effect is not ideal as you lose respect, trust, and connection to others. You can get a similar effect by calmly saying no. That still leaves us with the question of how we will reward the new, wanted response. Every time you respond rather than react, you could use the calmer situation itself as the reward.

Rewards work best when they are physical, sensory, and immediate. Examples of strong rewards include:

- Mental or emotional relief.
- Food or drink (taste).
- A nap (physical rest).
- An activity you like.
- A hug or cuddle (physical connection).
- Laughter.
- Positive attention or acclaim.

The more powerful the reward, the quicker the new behavior will become habitual.

Staying mindful of what it is you want to achieve is also needed. Remind and refocus yourself with a vision board, a quote or meme printed and stuck where you will see it, a reminder on device screens, a tactile or visual object that symbolizes what you want, or similar. At first, you will need some reminding and support, so sharing your goals with a helpful person is also a good idea. All of these things come together to make the new behavior more likely.

Lastly, there is no fixed timeline for how long this takes. It takes as long as it takes. It depends on how consistent you are, how powerful the reward is, and how strong the habit is that you are replacing. The 21-day myth is just that, a myth. Anyone who has gotten into the habit of smoking, for example, will know that the powerful reward of the rush and relaxed feeling of a smoke makes it a habit much faster than 21 days. That is not a habit you want to add into the mix, but understanding why some things become habits so quickly will help you understand how to replace, change, and create healthier, more useful behavior choices going forward.

What existing habits are contributing to your stress load? Prioritize them and get to work shifting them one by one.

Whether it is a habit of thought or deed, even small changes can bring a lot of relief. And each bit of relief and ease adds up until eventually you look back at how stressed you were from a much calmer, happier place and see how very far you have come.

6

DEALING WITH STRESS AT WORK

"My boss told me to have a good day. So I went home." - (Anon.)

We spend about a full third of our lives at work, one way or another. The sad thing is many of us fall into any paying job. We take whatever we can find and run with that. Many years can pass, spending precious hours of your life haphazardly, with paying your bills as your primary goal.

Honestly, of course, this is stressful. The endless jokes about Mondays and Fridays, annoying bosses and colleagues, and the inevitability of hating what you do for a living may be funny at first, but they hide a deeper, more painful truth.

Most of us are unhappy in our work life.

Many of us dream about walking out, winning the lottery, or for some other magical event that will make all of this go away. We live from weekend to weekend, holiday to holiday, and sometimes from sick day to sick day.

Yikes! Listen, if this is you, it has to stop right now.

I don't mean quit your job, necessarily. What I do mean is that a surprisingly few small changes to your thoughts and actions can make whatever your reality is a whole lot nicer and less stressful.

FINDING MEANING

If what you are doing daily, for a large part of your day, is not in some way purposeful, meaningful, or inspiring for you, you are going to battle. But just as we do not always know what is important to us, quite often, we haven't stopped to analyze what we do for a living in these terms either.

Yes, sure, if you are employed, the overall goal is to make money for whoever owns the business. But that is extremely simplistic and limited, to think that is the only reason your job exists. This industry, service, widget, or whatever it is, was chosen, at some point, because not only would it create an income, but also because it was linked to a talent or skill set, and that is often also linked to a person's values and interests.

Many business owners have other agendas over and above making money. They may have a social cause or idea they hold dear or a way of life or value they want to embody and share. Sometimes you will find this reflected in the company vision and mission statement if it is well written and updated. You will also see this in the pattern of choices made by those in power. What they do speaks way louder than what they say. So what are they doing day to day, for the little people and not just the ones they want to impress?

Sometimes you will find that their values are not at all aligned to your own, and that is probably a good time to start looking for another employment opportunity or risk increasing frustration and upset on your part and theirs.

But unless they are seriously lacking in ethics and integrity, you can generally find some good, helpful stuff somewhere in the mix. Is this stuff that aligns with you and that you can get behind? Who is benefiting from the service or product? How is it helping to improve the world? Take your current story about your job, and using the exercise around reframing stories we did earlier, see if you can rewrite it in a more positive and meaningful way, one that leaves you feeling good on some level about your part in it.

In a groundbreaking book, *Nine Lies About Work* by Marcus Buckingham and Ashley Goodall, they take a deeper look into what makes work either a good experience or a bad one. They also look at what makes a company successful because successful companies understand what is important and why for their human resource. They also get that they probably (definitely) would not make it at all without their team and key role players within the workforce.

The many systems, tools, and processes, the end-of-year parties, bonus cheques, increases, benefit packages, and so on are all great (of course, we all like them). But, that's not what makes work meaningful or why we are loyal, reliable, invested, or engaged with our jobs.

Buckingham and Goodall's work truths, based on extensive research, include the idea that:

- People don't work for companies but rather the team they are a part of because the connection and a feeling of belonging come from the people closest to you every day.
- It is not about goals. It is about meaning. People want to know why more than what.
- It is not about feedback and reviews. It is about attention. We want to be seen and heard, and celebrated.
- Achievements and productivity are not about potential so much as momentum.
- It is not work-life balance so much as love-in-work that matters.

These are the main ones that relate to you and your stress at work. There are four others you can read for yourself if you wish. Just in case you were wondering what happened to all nine.

This tells us that the meaning you find and the parts of your job that you enjoy are what you need to focus on if you want to start feeling better about it all. Perhaps this is what you create yourself. Perhaps it is found in how you treat customers and coworkers or the level and quality of service you give. Meaning does not have to come from above. You can make it happen based on what's important to you.

SELF-MANAGEMENT AND MOTIVATION

A lot of stress comes from deadlines and pressure from excessive workloads. With the neverending push to give 150%, to be better, do more, and so on, you can easily fall into the "when I get this done, then I can relax/be happy/satisfied" paradigm trap.

Using many of the concepts we have already discussed, like creating boundaries, focussing on the present moment, and dealing with frustration, are as useful in the workplace as anywhere. Maybe even more so.

But before we even start worrying about other people, we need to look at what is happening with ourselves.

Motivation comes with meaning. It also helps to organize your life a little. Creating momentum and consistent behavior is another way to bump this up a bit. Nike had it right when they said, "Just do it." You make steady progress by getting into certain behavioral habits at work and achieving set daily goals. How we do this comes down to a little bit of time management and self-management.

Practical Exercise: Time Awareness

To know how to improve your time management, you first need to understand how you are currently spending it. You may think you already know, but you would be mighty surprised to discover the truth. Most people are.

- Estimate what your average day includes and how much time you spend on each thing—for example, emails, phone calls, meetings, planning, projects, and so on.
- For a period of seven days, track your activity from waking to sleeping every 30 minutes or so. Be meticulous about this and don't just thumbsuck or estimate anything; otherwise, you will not make any helpful discoveries.
- Now analyze the data, and work out the average per activity by adding up all the minutes per activity and dividing it by the number of days you measured it all over. Exclude weekend or rest days, or work them out separately.
- How does what you estimated compare with reality? Is there anything you want to cut back on or do more of?
- Create a daily blueprint for your time based on what you want, and then stick to it as closely as possible going forward.

Sometimes you don't need to start out feeling that motivated; you just need to do the things. Break bigger tasks down into manageable sizes, pick the thing you feel the least resistant to, and get that done. Keep going. I don't know how many times I have put a task off, with stress building and the task growing in dimension and complexity in my mind, only to find on doing it that it is easier and goes quicker than I thought. And that means that a lot of time was wasted feeling anxious and procrastinating for nothing.

Make sure to work time for self-care and unproductive moments or interruptions. Don't force the issue if you aren't feeling it. But don't lose momentum either. Pick something else on the list to do and do it. Even completing a small task will create a feeling of confidence, achievement, and productivity. This feeling leads to the ability to do more and better as you go.

Lastly, don't be afraid to drop, defer, or delegate non-essential, non-urgent stuff. Ask or organize whatever extra help you may need. Suffering alone and under pressure, if no one knows that you need extra time, people, or other resources, is not helpful for anyone.

Learn to speak up, plan, and organize whatever is needed. I would rather my team do this than let me know at the last minute that a crucial deadline can't be met.

If you find you lack motivation, allow yourself to do something else for a while. Try something different or new, or a little bit creative, to help re-inspire you.

DEALING WITH CONFLICT AND DIFFICULT PEOPLE

So much unnecessary distress is caused by workplace conflict that can be avoided.

Some of the few tips that will ease workplace relations include:

- Staying calm and releasing emotions before you do or say something you will regret.
- Seeing other people's bad behavior as mainly to do with them and not you. Not taking it personally.
- Understanding that everyone is going through something. You don't know what that may be, so be kind. Assume the best, not the worst, wherever possible.
- Dropping your ego and keeping the desired outcome in mind throughout.
- Focussing on the problem behavior and not making things personal.

- Asking a lot of questions and listening fully.
- Getting as many facts as you can before deciding how to proceed.
- Putting plans in place for repeat problems. Agreeing with the other roleplayers if possible.
- See conflict as a positive force for change. If it is caught early enough and handled well, it can be the springboard for positive change and improved relationships.
- Don't let conflict fester and grow too solid and difficult to shift. This is when people and groups take sides, and all kinds of unfortunate and unhelpful stuff can unfold.

Understand that no matter what you do, there will be times you can't fix everything and times when people are that damaged or toxic that they behave truly horrendously.

In this case, you need to accept that ill-mannered, unaware, bullying, or insensitive people exist, and you can't change them. You get them everywhere, unfortunately. You need to recognize that this is what you are dealing with and come up with some contingencies.

Workplace bullies are just as common as playground bullies. You don't expect them because you think people should know better by adulthood. Sadly they don't. These are the ones to remove, avoid, and ignore as far as humanly possible. If that means turning off your cell phone after hours, moving their desk to the Outer Hebrides (if you have that power), or just keeping contact to a bare minimum, then that is what you do. If you are forced to have anything to do with them, keep very good records, and get witnesses. Build a case and, at some point, discuss this with human resources. Focus on the behavior and results rather than your dislike of the person.

All it takes is one bad apple to cut productivity off at its knees. Most places are growing to understand this and have a zero-tolerance policy for such nonsense. Of course, if the problem is the big boss, start sending out your CV because sticking around in a bad environment that will never change is poison for your heart, mind, and soul. It is simply not worth it.

These are all constructive steps to make your work life more pleasant, enjoyable, and stress-free. Also, having a few strong, reliable, trustworthy connections with people you feel safe, comfortable, and happy around is super helpful. Mentors, role models, and good friends are what make work a place you can look forward to being in.

7

STRESS AT HOME

"Sometimes life can be difficult. Life happens. From financial problems to struggling children to marital stress, a [person] could easily get bogged down in the day to day drudge" - Brooke Jorden.

Adding people always comes with added stress–if you let that be your reality. By the very nature of life, when you add in any potentially random factors outside of your control, you can find your days interrupted, distracted, filled with problems you did not create, and more. Depending on how reactive and easily frustrated you get, any amount of life, no matter how small, could drive you over the edge, no matter how small. Adding in people means adding in an even greater randomness factor, as they act on their environment (and you) more intentionally and unexpectedly than, say, a pet, or a shrub, or the weather, might.

It is very easy to be calm if you live all alone, in the middle of nowhere, with no one to bug you. And even then, if you are not truly calm and at peace, even the ants and birds will frustrate you.

The measure of true inner peace is when you can be in the

middle of many people amid chaos and be able to smile serenely and take the next measured step.

TWO EARS ONE MOUTH

"Any problem, big or small, within a family, always seems to start with bad communication. Someone isn't listening" - Emma Thompson.

Families tend to carry a lot of emotional and mental baggage. It is hard to avoid. You have generally spent a lot of time around each other, and they have seen you warts and all. That increases the chance that people get upset, conflict festers, and beliefs about each other become entrenched. There are often agendas, expectations, and issues that are never discussed constructively yet still inflict themselves on our lives in annoying ways.

It becomes a problem when you are forced to live in close quarters or spend time with people you don't feel happy around.

The best and pretty much only way to deal with this is to get talking. This solution does not mean that things will be perfectly resolved, but it raises the chances that some problems and conflicts can be eased. The more mutual understanding can be increased in both kind and compassionate ways, the better for everyone.

I know this may feel very hard if you have a traumatic or toxic history with someone. It takes a certain level of maturity and self-awareness, which not everyone will have. It takes forgiveness and insight into what is needed for the whole relationship going forward.

What outcome is needed?

- Do you need to share space or time with each other on a regular basis?
- Is it important to you that you maintain this relationship?

STRESS AND HOW TO MANAGE IT

If the answer is yes to either of these, then a few steps will need to be taken.

And core to this is getting communication flowing better.

- Stay calm. If a lot needs working through, it will not help to lose your cool at each small slight or frustration. Use time out, counting and breathing, and all the self-calming techniques you need.
- Do not emotionally attach to anything they think or do. Step back and get curious. Try to keep your ego out of it. Go for workable solutions wherever possible. Remember, you cannot make other people think or do anything. You need to work with and around others to find a way to manage the situation.
- Forgive and let go of the past as much as you can. This is for you and your peace of mind, not for anyone else. Also, allow for the possibility that people can learn, grow, and change for the better, just as you can. If someone shows improved behavior, appreciate and support that if you want to see more of it.
- When talking, be sure to listen way more than you speak. The whole two ears and one mouth story might be a bit simple, but it is still true. Listen at least twice as much as you speak, and listen with your full attention. Try to understand what they are saying from their point of view, and ask questions if you aren't sure. If someone is very emotional, let them get everything off their chest until you see they are feeling some level of release and ease. It is easier to communicate this way.
- We tend to treat those closest to us the worst. Turn this around. Your family is not your punching bag just because you feel safe or because you think they are stuck with you. They aren't. Just as you can form very close

bonds with people unrelated to you, so can blood relations become bitter enemies or disconnected from each other if they are pushed far enough. Your partner, kids, parents, and extended family can choose not to spend time around you if they are constantly made to feel bad by you. I guess my point is that you should never assume that family will always be there just because they are family.

You need to work on these relationships as hard as you do on those with your good friends. You need to be investing more positive than negative energy for family relationships to work.

- Always be kind and respectful. Even when others are losing it or behaving badly, you can help calm the situation by remaining calm and polite. A good guideline is the Buddhist three gates concept.

First, is what you are saying kind?
Is it true? How do you know?
Is it necessary? What are you hoping to achieve with your words?

- Be honest and authentic. Don't say what you think others want to hear. That communicates incorrect and unhelpful information. Speak your truth. Just do it nicely. So often, a person will share what's on their mind with me regarding their partners, parents, or kids, and one of my first questions is always, "Why don't you say what you have said to me, to them?" This is a good question to consider. Moving towards the truth means it becomes easier to understand and problem-solve.
- Steer clear of assumptions and always get as many

current facts as possible. Watch out for faulty thinking and negative biases. Don't expect people to read your mind. They really can't.

Sometimes it helps to set up sharing sessions with clear, agreed rules. For example, the old Native-American tradition of using a talking stick is one way to give everyone a fair chance to be heard without interruption.

And maybe sharing sessions need to be made more regular to avoid conflict and misunderstandings from becoming cemented in.

POSITIVE PARENTING

Experiencing a stress-free home life when small and growing children are involved takes some doing. Every child presents with a unique set of challenges and needs. Your level of stress may relate to how certain situations are managed, but it can also be heightened by extra parenting obstacles, like with a special needs child, for example. We don't get a perfect set of parenting skills with our new baby. We have to learn, and a lot of learning happens as the child grows. Our child becomes our teacher in many ways. If we can manage ourselves, be less reactive, and more responsive, and self-aware, we tend to manage a lot better.

Even if the child has some extra challenges, parental behavior can be adapted. A solution can be found that works for your specific situation. No child will behave perfectly all the time anyway, but it is all about how you handle whatever problem behavior occurs from day one.

Historically we have been taught that discipline means force, raised voices, and even physical punishment. While this may work short-term to get the behavior you want, it does not teach your child anything beyond fear, resistance, and disconnection. It breaks down the relationship, and the child, long term. It is abusive by its very nature, and what you end up with is a damaged child on one level or another. Parenting with fear means children are more likely to lie to you, hide important information from you, and resist and avoid you.

When they grow up, if this has been the modus operandi, don't be surprised if the kids don't want to stay in contact much.

It is tempting to resort to these measures when you are tired, overwhelmed, or stressed out, and we know that children pick the times when you are feeling like this to push your buttons. It isn't intentional. They often get scared when their important people are not doing so well. It is a survival response, as misguided as it seems. But we need to resist this fear-based stuff and develop a more workable and constructive way to deal with the stresses of parenting.

Parenting with love rather than fear is the answer. If we can ask ourselves what is behind our parenting choices and bring it back to these two options, it can help make things more transparent and easier to decide. Being aware and mindful of how you are parenting will help you avoid defaulting into bad habits that have perhaps been used on you and thus taught to you by your caregivers.

This does not mean you have no rules and let the children run riot. This can be a knee-jerk reaction to having an unhappy childhood yourself, but either extreme does not work well in the end.

Again, as with much of life, staying calm is the main thing. Losing your cool means that you are out of control, which means you can't make good decisions or parent that effectively.

Next, self-awareness is crucial. You need to be observing yourself and working on yourself. Because if your own life is a mess, that is what you are going to be modeling for your kids. Unfortunately, children do not learn much from what you say but from what you do. If you show the behavior you want from them, you are way more likely to get it in return. So many parents hold their children to such high standards of behavior, but if you observe the parents, they do not walk their talk. So check in with yourself on this issue. If you expect good manners, do you use them yourself?

In the first year of life, an infant needs a responsive parent who consistently meets their needs. It is intense to start with, but providing a stable, caring presence will establish a feeling of trust and security that allows them to be more independent later. It also influences how they relate to others. Keep your expectations aligned with the child's age and stage as well. The rough rule of thumb is five minutes per year of life possible for attention span, and of course, judging safety and ability. Don't expect a fish to climb a tree; you will be disappointed. Likewise, don't expect a child to do or be something way in advance of their years and skill level.

Let your children get involved with family life and chores. Slowly handing over increasingly complex responsibilities as they show they are able to take them on is part of raising responsible kids.

At the same time, the main way we learn is through trying, getting things wrong, self-correcting, and keeping on trying. So letting children try to do things for themselves before jumping in is a good thing, as long as they are safe doing so. That is how they build confidence and abilities and eventually become competent enough to be independent.

Communicating your expectations and boundaries, and house rules clearly and consistently is an important part of getting everyone to understand what is okay and not okay.

Teaching your children how to identify and manage their own emotions as they grow and teaching them the basics of self-awareness and self-care, which we touch on in this book, are all ways you slowly build a strong, happy family.

TOP CONFLICTS

The top conflicts at home are usually around money, chores, parenting styles, quality/family time, and sex.

"Most couples have not had hundreds of arguments; they've had the same argument hundreds of times" - Gay Hendricks.

Some of these arguments can fester and escalate. Sides are taken, lines are drawn, and repair and conciliation become unlikely over time. Relationship 'flu sets in, and everyone is increasingly miserable.

Keeping sight of what you first liked in each other can help. What value does each add to the other? What happiness is possible? What was the point of both of you getting together in the first place? Re-present yourselves to that.

Talking things out can help a lot. Use the guidelines given in that section to help you along. Checking your thinking for those faulty thinking traps is also really useful.

At the heart of many families, conflicts are someone doing something (or not doing something) that another expects. This comes down to expectations and how they are communicated and agreed upon.

It links back to the thought trap of false consensus. You think that people are both mind readers who think and feel the same way you do. You assume that because you want a thing, everyone will. Someone hit that game show buzzer because this is a major fail.

In every relationship, one of the first things to discuss is expectations. What do you want and expect from me, and what do I expect from you? Not only do these need to be shared, but they also need to be agreed to. Just because you have an expectation does not mean anyone has to conform to it. Sometimes you need to negotiate a compromise of some sort or barter deal where you each get to have certain things that you are responsible for and that you do alone. And it does not stop there because as the relationship grows and changes, and you, yourself, change, this conversation needs to be had on an ongoing basis.

In the end, the level of stress in the home and your personal relationships comes down first and foremost to your own self-awareness. Hard on its heels comes the ability to communicate, observe and manage your own thoughts, emotions and reactions.

8

DEALING WITH CHANGE

"Every great dream begins with a dreamer. Always remember, you have within you the strength, the patience, and the passion to reach for the stars to change the world." -Harriet Tubman.

Change can feel super scary and unwanted. Many of us push hard against it, resist and avoid it wherever possible. The thought of possible future changes sends us into complete worry and anxiety mode. We assume change will bring extra work, hardship, and maybe extra challenges. We don't know why, but it feels big and problematic.

The thing is that change is pretty inevitable. Our lifestyles, workplaces, technology, relationships, and every part of our lives are subject to continual change. It may be small stuff, but it is happening. And it adds up.

If we choose to ignore it, we are burying our heads in the sand, and at some point, a large, sharp-toothed beast is going to bite at our exposed bottoms.

Rather than spending all our energy resisting what is truly inevitable, it is less stressful and more logical to accept what is and put our energy into being aware, responsive, and adaptive. It is those who adapt who survive.

COMFORT ZONES

We find ourselves in a nice, comfy situation but over time, things change (because they always do). What happens then is that our comfort zone starts getting increasingly uncomfortable. And yet we stick with what we know because it is familiar and somehow comforting, if not comfortable.

For example, a couple who have both changed over the years and no longer see eye-to-eye stay in the relationship with no effort to change their expectations or relationship skills. They are both increasingly unhappy but just continue with the status quo.

A person stays in a job they increasingly dislike because they feel safe knowing what they are doing there and might not cope in a new job.

Someone stays in a neighborhood that is slowly deteriorating and growing increasingly unsafe. The thought of finding a new home, uplifting, moving, finding new shops and travel routes feels like too much change.

I could go on. I am sure we all have experienced a range of these situations before.

One surefire way to know that you are in a comfort zone is when you notice increasing discomfort in familiar situations. This may take the form of increasing frustration and conflict, or you may feel bored, tired, and lackluster. Perhaps you find yourself avoiding elements of the current situation. If you find excuses and lack confidence, you may be stuck in a state of fear. And fear is at the core of an unhealthy and unhelpful approach to change.

You have two options when you are stuck in a comfort zone. You can either stay where you are, in which case eventually things will get so uncomfortable the situation becomes unmanageable.

You end up having a breakdown, and then hopefully a breakthrough. Then you make a bunch of changes, and afterward, you experience a great deal of ease and flow. You wonder why you didn't make these changes before, but your avoidance in dealing with change may very well mean this cycle happens all over again.

The other, slightly better option is to be aware and responsive to changes happening in and around you. Watch out for signs of an increasing unhealthy comfort zone situation. Stay as flexible as possible in your habits, choices, and thinking. By living in the present moment and engaging fully with whatever is happening, rather than interacting based on past information, you also stand a better chance of being constructively responsive to change. Dealing with challenges that arise rather than ignoring and avoiding them is part of this.

To level this up even further, you can start looking for current and future trends at work, at home, and in your world in general, and begin planning small shifts in your behavior and choices based on these. In those parts of your life where you feel some fear, allow yourself to try out small changes or new things. You don't need to go too big with this. Small, incremental moves outside of your comfort zone add up to consistent, positive changes in the long run. This is the best way to avoid getting stuck with stale and increasingly limiting situations. If something makes you feel a little uncomfortable and is not dangerous or harmful to you or others, challenge yourself to try it out. Do small test runs in a controlled environment.

Looking for meaning and purpose, staying present to your values, pursuing things that excite and inspire you, and setting new goals will all contribute to a positive change mentality.

Another way to keep things fresh, and stimulate memory and brain function too (by the way), is to mix things up. Try out new foods, new travel routes, speak to people you would not normally interact with, watch new movies, learn new things, and work at replacing unwanted habits. This keeps you more in a growth zone and helps you stay flexible about change on the whole. The more you stick to the same old same old, stuck with familiar patterns and situations, the harder it is to deal with a changing environment.

We do this more flexibly within a business environment, although the long string of giant corporations who have folded because they couldn't deal with change is also pretty long.

Now is a good time for you to think about those times you might have been stuck in a comfort zone in your life. Did you realize what was happening in time, or did things have to get a lot worse before you eventually made a change? Are there any current situations where you feel stale, bored, and frustrated? Maybe it is time to shake things up a bit?

Practical Exercise: Riding the Wave

- What areas in your life feel boring or meaningless?
- What new behavior or learning can you try in these areas?
- Where do you feel some fear in your life?
- What needs to shift, or what can you do to feel less fear?

Make a shortlist of new ideas or behaviors to try out. What is the worst that can happen if you do this? If that happens, what can you do?

Reframing the story we tell ourselves about change is also helpful for reducing inner resistance. You already know how to reframe and rewrite the narrative, but here are some suggestions around what you are telling yourself about it.

There is no reason to think I will not be fine going forward. I have survived everything in my life so far.
I am ready for whatever life brings.
I choose to accept change.
Change brings good things.
Change brings me closer to success and happiness every day.
Change provides new opportunities for me.
Change has made me who I am today.
I accept what I can't control. I can handle it.
Although these changes may feel less than ideal, I am okay.
I create change so that change does not bring me down.
I am free to change my life whenever and however I want.

By telling yourself it is okay, it automatically becomes easier to deal with. It helps redirect your energy into taking constructive actions that support the growth you need to survive in a changing world.

BUILDING RESILIENCE IN A CHANGING ENVIRONMENT

Fear is at the root of our resistance to change. So by reducing our fears, we can go a long way towards feeling a lot better and stronger. It redirects our energies from fear-based reactivity and avoidance into the present and future-oriented action.

When we are in reaction to change and stressing out, we tend to stop doing all of those things we desperately need to do to deal with life. It is vital at these times that we make time to eat properly, exercise, and watch our sleep quality. It may feel like wading through mud, but self-care is imperative. Just as you would calmly but firmly insist that a little kid having a meltdown takes a nap, eats something healthy, and so on, you need to almost parent yourself through these tough times. Try to re-establish normal routines as far as possible. Work some downtime and pleasure into your day wherever you can. Just because life is tough right now does not mean it has to be totally miserable.

Get to the gym, take a nature walk, watch a good movie, read a book that is amusing and distracting, or make yourself a delicious meal.

When things feel like they are falling apart, take some time out. Do some fear-setting exercises. Tim Ferris is well-known for his fear processing methods, which in simple terms is just listing what you are worried about, looking at worst-case scenarios, and making plans for each possible consequence helps reduce the power of the unknown and ease stress levels. If you have a plan, it makes it way less scary.

If you know change is coming up, spending some time brainstorming what can be done, who could help, and what might be needed brings it all into the realm of the known and doable.

Reflect on past events that may be similar and what worked and did not work. Keep your focus on what is going right once you have done what you can about what is going wrong.

Redirecting our energy helps us become way more resilient.

CONCLUSION

"We can easily manage if we will only take, each day, the burden appointed to it. But the load will be too heavy for us if we carry yesterday's burden over again today, and then add the burden of the morrow before we are required to bear it." – John Newton.

How we choose to manage our emotions, thoughts, and resulting choices is going to decide whether we lead stressed out, unhappy lives plagued with anxiety, stress-related health problems, and constant upset, or we calm the whole deal down.

This is a clear decision we need to take to say, "Enough is enough." There is no reason why we need to live rushing from thing to thing, swamped in frustration, resentment, and pressure.

I have lived that way, and it sucks. Luckily I eventually worked out ways to improve the quality of my life and calm things down. My out-of-control stress levels were having a horrible impact on my health, my family, my work colleagues, and my peace of mind. I was almost permanently irritated and reactive and resorted to endless cups of coffee in the day and wine or medication at night to try dialing out and down. My diet, exercise, and self-care, in

CONCLUSION

general, were virtually non-existent. Sure I was earning very well and managing a home, parenting, and a workplace, but I never felt like I was fully present or good at any of it–a calamity waiting to happen. It took burnout and several breakthroughs for me to accept that things had to change.

My story does not need to be yours. And if it already is, it is still not too late to turn things around.

The first rule of the stressless club is to notice what is going on with yourself. Understanding how our brains and bodies are programmed to respond to our environment is a great start. Your thoughts, feelings, and physical state need to be watched. They are all important signs as to what is going on with you.

The second rule is to get moving and work those fight-or-flight chemicals out of your system as quickly as possible. In fact, this should be the first rule, but some of us are so disconnected or busy rushing around that we forget even to notice what is happening within our own bodies and minds.

I have learned that when I am stressed, I get a few sharper slaps from the universe if I have missed noticing it. These take the form of an aching jaw muscle, from clenching my teeth, and also a sudden clumsiness. I get snagged on cupboard doors or front door handles, drop things and break things. At some point, generally, when cursing the door handle and trying to retrieve my favorite sweater that has now been torn, realization crashes in. I have not been paying attention, and I am rushing way too much. This is the time to stop, take a breath, and ground myself. If necessary, I will even stop myself, keys in hand, at the front door, and do a few minutes of breathing work. I present myself in the moment by doing a sensory exercise, and only when I feel fully earthed will I allow myself to continue with my day. It is a sure recipe for a later disaster if I don't do this.

Self-care is the third rule of the stressless club. When I notice I am feeling more stressed than usual, I reflect on what I am doing or not doing. I will often come up with some pretty obvious answers, like that sixth cup of coffee I drank on that deadline day yesterday, the lack of sleep that followed, or the fact that I haven't exercised or even taken a moment outdoors in my peaceful garden for days. Duh! This is time to get things back on track and quickly. It does not matter how crazy things are; you must take time to fix these basics. If you don't, it will only make things harder for you. It's just not worth skipping it.

The fourth rule of the stressless club is to simplify whatever you can, especially if you are feeling breathless and overwhelmed. Simplifying by dropping, deferring, or delegating can provide immediate relief. Don't underestimate how effective a quick re-arrangement of workload and scheduling can be, and don't overestimate how crucial your presence or service delivery is either. There are plenty of 'indispensable' people six feet under, and amazing how magically lives go on, and people make alternative arrangements once they have to. It helps to keep this in perspective.

Always come back to what you want and what is truly important in this moment, and get very clear on this. It helps when you have to say no to all the less important stuff.

It is also better to simplify as you go along than to do so when things get to boiling point. But if that pressure cooker is steaming, release some pressure as soon as possible. It doesn't help to put workload, other people's agendas, needs, or commitments ahead of your mental and physical health. If you burn out and lose the plot, none of these things can happen anyway, and quite likely, you will lose more time at that stage too. It pays to do what is needed now, to save lengthy recovery periods and serious damage control later.

The fifth rule of the stressless club is letting go of the past and keeping your mind from too many future forays. Bringing your attention back to this present moment, where life is happening, and where you can find absolute joy, love, meaning, and peace is

CONCLUSION

one of the most crucial and valuable skills you can develop in this lifetime. Living in the past that leads to things like guilt and overthinking, and living in the future leads to worry, anxiety, and fear.

The sixth rule is to watch your thoughts. Catch that negative inner critic and turn those words around. Use positive, supportive, and kind words to and for yourself. Reframe stressful and depressing life narratives into more powerful, self-affirming ones wherever you can. Do not underestimate the power of where you put your focus, either. Focussing on a bunch of fears, worries, unhappy memories, or similar is pointless unless you are there to resolve them once and for all. Keeping your focus mainly on your strengths, successes, gratitude for life, and all the good things will make you stronger, calmer, and happier. This does not mean avoiding feelings or problems or squashing your emotions. That way lies toxic and destructive false positivity. Engage with the hard stuff, use your emotions as the messengers, and then move on to nicer things.

The seventh rule is to build stress release into your daily self-care regimen. Don't skip it. Be ruthless about it. Taking time to meditate, exercise, journal, reflect, take that aromatherapy bath, play your favorite music, play a game, have a laugh, and connect with the important people in your life is not selfish. It is necessary. And while we are on the subject, drop the useless narrative about selfishness. Taking care of yourself and your happiness is vital, not optional. Anyone who tells you you are selfish for doing so has their own selfish agenda that you are interfering with. Be alert and work those boundaries.

That's the eighth rule of the stressless club. Say no. Say it nicely and politely, but say it often. Practice saying it in the mirror or with small things if big "no's" feel awkward. Work your way up to the confidence for the bigger ones. If you don't, you will find yourself living other people's lives and agendas, and you will lose your sense of identity, and your mind, along the way.

CONCLUSION

Watch out for the bullies and less conscious people who would run right through and over you if it served their purposes. Put your defenses and systems in place to protect yourself or avoid such people altogether.

The ninth rule is to observe where you invest your emotional energy. Only put it into the things that truly matter, and even then curate how much, how, and when.

Lastly, get good at dealing with change. Because that is what life is all about to a large degree. Change and our reaction to it. Embrace change as an opportunity to discover new things about yourself and the world and continually improve your life. Even if it feels hard at the moment, finding the lesson and the opportunities will make whatever you are going through easier to process. That is my final and tenth rule. Neat, right?

We are human beings, not human doings. Stop, assess where you are, and start living the lovely, peaceful, meaningful life you deserve, changing your quality of life and that of everyone who has to interact with you. You will naturally and organically become a much better person to be around, work with and live with. And your children will learn a bunch of good things from your great example.

Don't be that person who looks back on a long, rushed life and wonders what happened? Take your finger off the fast forward button and start living and living well. Everything I have shared with you here has been with that in mind. I hope you have taken the time to do the exercises here too, because that will give you more time in the long run.

I hope you have enjoyed this journey with me, that you are thoroughly armed and equipped for the quality of life you desire, and that the rest of your path will be one that doesn't even register that insidious word, stress.

REFERENCES

Ask the scientists. Ask The Scientists. (2020, April 2). Retrieved January 8, 2022, from https://askthescientists.com/

Buckingham, M., & Goodall, A. (2019). Nine lies about work. Summary of Nine Lies About Work by Marcus Buckingham and Ashley Goodall | Summaries.Com. Retrieved January 8, 2022, from https://summaries.com/blog/nine-lies-about-work

Clear, J. (2018, July 20). How willpower works: How to avoid bad decisions. James Clear. Retrieved January 8, 2022, from https://jamesclear.com/willpower-decision-fatigue

Gupta, R. (1349). Between music and medicine. Www.ted.com. https://www.ted.com/talks/robert_gupta_between_music_and_medicine?referrer=playlist-how_music_affects_us#t-249204

REFERENCES

Holmes, T. H., & Rahe, R. H. (1967). The social readjustment rating scale. Journal of Psychosomatic Research, 11(2), 213–218. https://doi.org/10.1016/0022-3999(67)90010-4

Li, Q. (2018, May 1). "Forest Bathing" Is Great for Your Health. Here's How to Do It. Time. https://time.com/5259602/japanese-forest-bathing/

MacKay, J. (2021, February 9). Context switching: Why jumping between tasks is killing your productivity. RescueTime Blog. Retrieved January 8, 2022, from https://blog.rescuetime.com/context-switching/

Nunner, M. (2021, March 16). Sound therapy and well-being: Some scientific studies. MedicinaNarrativa.eu. Retrieved January 8, 2022, from https://www.medicinanarrativa.eu/sound-therapy-and-well...

Stuart, A. (n.d.). Herbs, Vitamins, and Supplements Used to Enhance Mood. WebMD. https://www.webmd.com/diet/features/herbs-vitamins-and-supplements-used-to-enhance-mood#4

Thoma, M. V., La Marca, R., Brönnimann, R., Finkel, L., Ehlert, U., & Nater, U. M. (2013). The Effect of Music on the Human Stress Response. PLoS ONE, 8(8), e70156. https://doi.org/10.1371/journal.pone.0070156

Walsh, C. (2020, February 27). How scent, emotion, and memory are intertwined - and exploited. Harvard Gazette. Retrieved January 8, 2022, from https://news.harvard.edu/gazette/story/2020/02/how-scent-emotion-and-memory-are-intertwined-and-exploited/

REFERENCES

Wim Hof Method. (n.d.). Regular ice baths. Wim Hof Method. Retrieved January 8, 2022, from https://www.wimhofmethod.com/regular-ice-baths

ABOUT THE AUTHOR

Lori Maxwell was born in Sydney, Australia with a serious case of 'Itchy Feet'. She spread her wings after her schooling and initial further education and relocated to England, where she thrived.

Lori's career path has been varied with the constant theme of helping others. She's a magnet to those who seek advice. Her early life was challenging, and her time spent living in Southern Africa provided further insights into human nature and 'how the other half live'.

Lori has returned to Australia to live for a while. She is equally happy surrounded by friends & family at home for a meal, weekend rides on her motorbike with her husband or at the beach for walks and a long swim.

Lori hopes to help and inspire new generations through her writing.

Made in United States
Orlando, FL
13 May 2025